Arizona Twilight Tales

Arizona Twilight Tales

GOOD GHOSTS, EVIL SPIRITS & BLUE LADIES

Jane Eppinga

PRUETT PUBLISHING COMPANY
BOULDER, COLORADO

Printed in the United States of America

09 08 07 06 05 04 03 02 01 00 5 4 3 2 1

Library of Congress Cataloging-in-Publication Data
Eppinga, Jane, 1936–
Arizona twilight tales : good ghosts, evil spirits
& blue ladies / Jane Eppinga.
  p. cm.
Includes bibliographical references.
ISBN 0-87108-901-7 (alk. paper)
1. Ghosts—Arizona. 2. Ghost stories, American—Arizona.
3. Tales—Arizona.   I. Title.
BF1472.U6 E66 2000
133.1'09791—dc21   00-032353

Book design by Julie Noyes Long
Book composition by Lyn Chaffee
Cover art by Robert Chapman

Table of Contents

Acknowledgments, vii

Introduction, ix

Chapter 1—*Borderland Ghosts*, 1

Chapter 2—*Quest for the Soul*, 15

Chapter 3—*Phantoms of the Desert*, 25

Chapter 4—*On the Road Again*, 35

Chapter 5—*Evil Spirits*, 43

Chapter 6—*The Wishing Shrine*, 53

Chapter 7—*For Sojourners in Search*, 63

Chapter 8—*From the Ground Up*, 75

Chapter 9—*Native American Spirits*, 91

Chapter 10—*Military Ghosts*, 105

Chapter 11—*Arizona Bedeviled*, 115

Chapter 12—*La Llorona*, 123

Chapter 13—*The Blue Nun*, 133

Chapter 14—*The Miracle of the Roses*, 145

References, 153

Acknowledgments

First of all, thanks must go to the many fine historical organizations that supplied material for the book. They include the Southwest Folklore Center in Special Collections at the University of Arizona; the Arizona Historical Society with its four chapters in Tucson, Phoenix, Yuma, and Flagstaff; and the Arizona State Archives.

Betty Lane and Mary Bingham, from the Tubac Historical Society, did a fantastic job supplying books, articles, and other documentary materials. They always kept a pleasant demeanor and an active interest in my *Arizona Twilight Tales* project. Lori Davisson, retired Arizona Historical Society historian, shared her knowledge of Apache ghost stories and insights into the Apache understanding of ghosts. George Gaylord related his experience with the ghost at the Cochise Hotel.

Carolyn O'Bagy Davis gave information gleaned from her love of the Lady of Guadalupe. Alex Garcia gave freely of the material that he has collected over the years on La Llorona and other haunts of the Hispanic milieu. Betty Leavengood, always an encouraging friend, provided her interview of the descendants of the Aguirre family, who homesteaded the Buenos Aires Ranch. She also shared her knowledge of the Kentucky Camp ghost.

Pat Etter, archivist with the Carl Hayden Library, Arizona State University at Tempe, provided material on the folklore of houses in the Phoenix area. Carol Osman Brown shared her story of the Frank Luke house in Phoenix. Loren Wilson, volunteer at the Mohave County Historical Society, provided stories surrounding military figures. Nick Bleser told me about the ghost in his own haunted Tubac house.

Special thanks must go to the editor, Erin Murphy, who kept me on the straight ghostly path with meticulous editing, and also to copy editor

Laurian Escalanti. No book would see the light of day without a publisher such as Jim Pruett. Thanks to production editor, Kim Adams, and typesetter, Lyn Chaffee.

Orchids to the many friends who said, "Have you heard about the ghost at . . . ?" Well yes I did and here it is.

Spirits make their short appearances at sundown, and disappear as wispy tendrils of air when the sun rises. I'm just glad they stay around long enough to provide a few good stories.

Every effort has been made to verify the sites. However, gentle reader, remember that urban renewal, roads, and progress destroy ghost habitations, forcing the spirits to move on. Got to go now. I think a horseman just rode past my door. Funny, I don't see anything. Oh there he is and oh my goodness! He only has half a face.

Introduction

Yesterday upon the stair
I saw a man who wasn't there
I saw that man again today
I wish that man would go away.
                                    —Unknown

We feel so safe during the day as we go about our work, send our children off to school, and enjoy the outdoors—yet when the last rays of the sun disappear over the horizon, we call our children inside, turn on the lights, and lock the doors. We do this mostly to keep out robbers and hoodlums, but we also want to ignore the surrounding darkness. It is in the darkness that we see the shapes of those long-gone souls—some friendly, and some the very essence of evil. These shapes we call ghosts, tommyknockers, revenants, haunts, spooks, specters, or simply spirits, are the subject of *Arizona Twilight Tales*.

It should come as no surprise that Arizona has a respectable array of ghosts. When the Spaniards arrived in this area, they brought with them not only the Catholic religion, but also the popular folk practices of sixteenth-century Spain, which allow for close communion with the dear departed. These Spanish customs found fertile ground in Mexico and flourished in Arizona. On *Día de los Muertos*, the Day of the Dead, families make *pan del muerto* (dead man's bread) and gather at cemeteries to weep, laugh, feast with each other, and remember their dead.

Long after the Spanish conquistadors had come and gone, Arizona saw an influx of prospectors and preachers, miners and madmen, gamblers and soiled doves, all willing to flout the laws of God and the U.S. Constitution. Most searched for fortune but found nothing more than their own graves, and even then, some refused to stay put. Between dusk and dawn their spirits cross over and scare the bejammers out of ordinary folk.

When we hear the word *ghost,* we often think of white-sheeted wraiths, hell-bent on destroying us, but often they are merely revenants, or returners, who wander the earth, trying to complete unfinished business. In Arizona, one ghost carries a stolen toe to be returned to its owner, another has a revelation of hidden treasure that he could not claim for himself, and many seek revenge for an untimely death.

Not all ghosts are people. Arizona spooks include a ship, a mission church, and a train, the last of which periodically rescues people dying of thirst in the barren Willcox Playa, a prehistoric lakebed.

Native American ghosts are among Arizona's most ancient haunts. Navajo skinwalkers assume animal forms at night before perpetrating their mischief. For almost two hundred years the good Navajo spirit, *Begashibito,* has been helping lost travelers of every walk of life.

Tucson is populated with an abundance of city ghosts. Cloven-hoofed men lure young girls into their dances of death, and priests hold wild beasts at bay with crosses. These evil specters leave behind the sulfurous stench reminiscent of fire and brimstone.

Near Tucson, *El Tejano,* "the Texan," was betrayed by a comrade and shot to death in a posse ambush. His violent spirit stands guard over his fortune, stashed in a cave on Cat Mountain. His cache is still out there, but a terrible stipulation exists for those who would take his treasure: They must take it all or die. El Tejano cackles his ghastly laugh and roars, "*Todo o nada*" (all or nothing). Be warned that as quickly as you pick up a piece of gold, another piece appears.

Arizona has many military ghosts, among them an unusually tall soldier, wearing high boots and a uniform, who appeared one night in 1900 to disturb people living near the old Fort Lowell ruins. When residents attempted to exterminate the phantom, he faded into the adobe walls, where he presumably remains.

Every Arizona mining town worth its salt has a profusion of ghosts hanging out in saloons, abandoned glory holes, and red light cribs. Saloon frequenters see ghosts more clearly than the rest of us. Stories of tommy-knockers thrive in the honeycombed mine shafts. According to Cornish legend, they hide in the cracks and crevices to warn miners of impending danger—if they think the miners are worth saving.

You can't get your kicks on Route 666 anymore because this stretch of Arizona highway was renamed U.S. Route 191. Certain reports indicate that nothing much is different since the name change. Over the years many people have seen Satan standing at the side of the road with a pitchfork—a most useful tool for puncturing tires.

Arizona even boasts a headless and footless *gaberlunzie*. The gaberlunzie, a Scottish beggar, prowls a road near Tubac.

Finally, three powerful feminine spirits—La Llorona, the Blue Nun, and Our Lady of Guadalupe—complete our twilight tales. Their stories were born in Mexico but spread throughout the Americas. One committed a heinous crime, infanticide, while the other two are pure goodness.

The legend of *La Llorona*, "the wailing woman," has endured the centuries, with almost as many versions as there are tellers. She has been seen in Arizona, Texas, New Mexico, and Mexico, but always near water. She carries a burden of eternal punishment. She tried to enter heaven but was denied admittance until she rescues her drowned children.

The Blue Nun is a bilocator ghost. While most of us sometimes wish we could be in two places at once, bilocators transport their spirits over several thousand miles. Parapsychologists reluctantly agree this is possible but do not speak out on the matter.

Our Lady of Guadalupe helps the poor and downtrodden. Her radiant form is seen on everything from low rider cars to great cathedrals. She is the protectress of the Americas.

These stories did not happen to me personally, but I know people whose dear departed aunts, grandmothers, or other relatives or acquaintances had dealings with each of these spirits. Do not be too hasty to discredit Arizona ghosts. You may be one of the chosen few who makes a personal acquaintance with one. If you are, don't be frightened. They are a harmless lot—usually.

chapter 1

Borderland Ghosts

Small isolated mining and ranching communities such as Nogales, Tubac, Lochiel, Bisbee, and Douglas, characterize the Arizona-Mexico border. The 1882 Great Register of Cochise County reveals that its voters were born in Algiers, Argentina, Australia, Azores, Belgium, Brazil, Chile, Finland, French Guinea, Greece, Peru, Poland, Portugal, Russia, Slavonia, and Spain, and at sea. These ethnic cultures would forever leave their stamp on Arizona's history—and on its ghosts, as well.

Before television and the internet, the time after work was reserved for storytelling. Twilight was the time for telling about miracles, ghosts, La Llorona, headless horsemen, lost treasures, strange lights, the Devil tree, and the *gaberlunzie*—a Scottish mendicant, with neither hands nor feet, that trudges along the road between Nogales and Tubac at night, searching for what, no one knows. Twilight is the time when the night begins to pull the spirits who have rested during the day into our world.

In the seventeenth century, Spanish conquistadors captured what is now Arizona, New Mexico, and Mexico for the crown, while intrepid Spanish priests established a string of missions through the same lands for the cross. Along the borderlands, San Xavier del Bac still serves the Tohono O'odhams, and Tumacacori, no longer a church, is now part of the National Park Service. All that remains of other Arizona missions are crumbling ruins.

You say you don't believe in ghosts. Well then, try to explain to me those flickering distant lights over the Mission San Jose del Tumacacori and Tubac, which once served as a Spanish royal presidio. Two of Tumacacori's early priests, Fathers Balthazar Carrillo and Narciso Gutierrez, have long been moved from its cemetery to the cemetery of San Xavier del Bac near Tucson. However, every year on San Juan's Day, June 24, ghosts of these priests return to Tumacacori to tend the mission gardens. One of them, no one is sure which, reappears at midnight to say Mass.

A ghost is also associated with a bell that once hung in the Tumacacori mission. The bell, dedicated to San Antonio, was knocked out of the tower by lightning in 1848. Around the same time, the mission was largely abandoned, and folklore says that three Native Americans—a young sergeant; his wife, Margarita; and her brother—were chosen to bury the church's silver crucifix, chalice, and candlesticks under the mission floor for safekeeping.

One day many years later two bishops from Mexico City and their retinue of servants arrived at Tumacacori. They immediately ordered their servants to dig in front of the altar. As the hole got deeper and deeper, two old Indians came in to watch. Not realizing that these were two of the people who had buried the artifacts, the bishops ordered them to leave. As night came, work ceased. The bishops rolled up in their blankets and went to sleep.

Just before dawn they were awakened by the sound of digging. They looked up just in time to see the two old Indian men stick something under their serapes, jump on their horses, and leave. The bishops gave chase but were not a match for horsemen. Upon their return to Tumacacori, they examined the hole and discovered the imprint of a cross. The two men died many years later, but they never told Margarita where they re-buried the artifacts. Her ghost still wanders the countryside searching.

Around the turn of century, Henry Perkins camped in the abandoned Tumacacori mission one night with several cowboys and their horses and cattle. Though they found the church interior dark and forbidding, with moonlight producing eerie streaks along the nave's walls, the men were weary from roundup, and within a few minutes they had a fire going under their coffee, beans, and dried beef.

Tendrils of smoke curled to the ceiling. Firelight flickered on the walls. Moonlight cast the men's long shadows over the floor where worshippers had once knelt—at least, they thought the shadows were theirs. All refrained from voicing their discomfort as they consumed their dinner, ducking as bats swooped over them and fluttered out the door and windows. Having been up most of the past night and ridden all day long, the cowboys were bone weary. After seeing to their stock, they spread a bundle of straw on the mission floor and covered it with their saddle blankets. Soon they were fast asleep, but not for long.

Perkins was awakened by someone clutching his shoulder. A skull grinned from a niche in the wall where there should have been a saint, and a voice whispered, *"Mirad por dios."* In a show of bravado, one cowboy took it down and stuck a cigarette in its gaping mouth. The others drew back and refused to touch it.

They fell asleep again, but this time Perkins was awakened by pealing bells. The fire had gone out and the moon had disappeared behind the mountains, yet the room glowed with a yellow light that cast no shadows. The cowboys sat up in their bedrolls, staring at the chancel through glassy eyes. As Perkins turned toward the altar, his hair stood on end, his heart pounded, and his forehead broke out in a clammy sweat.

The chancel was filled with purplish light. From off in the distance came the sound of a soft, low chant bubbling like a distant stream. It grew louder and louder and until it swelled into a rich, primeval hymn, familiar yet foreign. A robed priest appeared, swaying censers, an acolyte on either side of him. Incense rose and hovered above the three figures like halos. From the mist emerged a snake with the face of an old man, full of compassion and sorrow. The priest knelt, rose, and knelt again while the acolytes drifted out through the mist.

Perkins tried to call out, but no voice came. Dark, melancholy silhouettes slowly drifted in and filled the church, where they assumed human shapes and knelt on the floor. The chanting started again. The priest rose, raising his hands to the heavens as if invoking a blessing. The kneeling forms dropped lower and lower until they dissipated into the floor. When the chanting ceased, a mighty shriek rent the air.

The cowboys collapsed, senseless, and did not awaken again until sunrise. Afterwards, only Perkins would speak of that terrifying night, but it is said that the life of every man there was inexorably affected by it. A few even gave up drinking for a couple of days.

From 1777 to 1779, pioneer priests established a string of small chapels near present-day Yuma along the Colorado River, and for awhile it seemed they would enjoy success with the Yuma Indians. The Yumans, however, rebelled and torched the chapels. In a hail of arrows and axes, they massacred Fathers Francisco Garces, Juan Diaz, Joseph Matias Moreno, and Juan Antonio Barreneche along with converted Indians, among them many women and children.

They kidnapped two small children, a boy and a girl, and took them to their camp along the Colorado River. That night, these children woke screaming and pointing to the bluff on the other side of the river. The Yumans stared in horror as four robed figures walked in the moonlight, each carrying a lighted candle, just as the padres did during vespers.

Immediately, the Yumans moved their camp farther away from the haunted spot. However, whenever they came in sight of the destroyed mission, apparitions of the holy ones solemnly walking to mass reminded them of their heinous deed. On moonlit nights these robed figures are still seen solemnly carrying candles along the mountain ledges.

Ghosts haunt many of the old borderland ranches. The Buenos Aires ranch, now a private preserve, once belonged to Pedro Aguirre. Its great hacienda is worthy of a romantic Spanish love ballad. The vast ranch also had a schoolhouse, cooks' quarters, post office, and customs station, along with rooms that were rented out to wealthy eastern dudes.

Modern-day visitors to the ranch sometimes hear the sounds of a rocking chair and rustling skirts on the porch during the night. When they look out, no one is on the porch, but the rocking chair is moving back and forth. There is no wind to explain it. The Aguirre family believes that it is Anna Maria Redondo, Pedro's first wife, who comes back to rock her children to sleep.

On one of the smaller ranches in the borderlands lived a poor widower, José, and his lovely daughter, Maria. José wanted nothing more than the best for his daughter. Most of all, he wanted her to marry well. But Maria fell in love with a poor cowboy, Juan, who worked as a vaquero on a big ranch.

One day José took Juan aside and said, "I forbid you to see my daughter. She must marry someone worthy, not the likes of a poor vaquero who only serenades her with beautiful words."

Juan said, "No matter what happens, I will serenade Maria at night."

That night Maria heard Juan singing "*Cucuru Cu Cu Paloma*," a beautiful ballad of a dove who has lost his love. When she looked out of the window, she could not see him.

She called her father and asked him, "Where is Juan?"

The father, too, heard the plaintive melody. He turned pale and said, "This cannot be."

Maria asked, "Why?"

"Because," he answered, "this morning I killed him."

In November of 1918, Carmen Zepeda built a trading post and homesteaded about three hundred acres between Tubac and Tumacacori on U.S. 89. She named the small community Carmen, and for awhile was its sole resident.

Even as the community grew, Carmen maintained complete control. She carried credit at the store for awhile if a family had hard times, but idlers paid up before they got another bite. Girls in Levis were not allowed in the store, and she never sold cigarettes to girls, even when they came back from college. She refused to sell liquor to anyone she thought had already imbibed too much. If a drunk got rowdy, she knocked him up the side of his head and took him into the store until he sobered up and apologized.

She ran cattle on her ranch and sold beef, and she built houses to rent out. In one of the houses lived a couple with a six-year-old daughter. One night after the mother and father put the child to bed, their dog barked louder than usual. Their daughter let out a terrified scream. They found her trembling and pointing toward the window. They saw nothing, but when they asked her what was the matter, she claimed that she had been awakened by a ghostly golden glow coming through the window. She had seen a face with hollow eye sockets. When she shrieked, the apparition faded from view.

Her parents agreed that she must have had a nightmare, but to be on the safe side, the father took a flashlight and searched the premises. He found nothing. Still, he felt a sense of something not quite right and a heaviness in the night air.

During the night the mother decided to check on the child. She froze in terror when she saw a strange yellow specter materialize through the closed window. What she saw might aptly be described as great balls of fire. Her scream woke the child and the father.

The mother grabbed a crucifix and made the sign of the cross. Slowly the specter drifted out of the window. The family rushed to look out and saw it hover briefly before disappearing in the west.

In the 1950s, at the age of 92, Carmen sold the store and moved to Nogales. A few years later she died. Thereafter, the new store owners saw a wispy figure of a woman from time to time. One day a dime dropped from the ceiling in front of the owner. Strange noises came from the living quarters behind the store, and thumping boots crossed the living room floor. Light bulbs in the bathroom inexplicably came unscrewed. Clothes hanging in the living room swung back and forth, even when there was no breeze. The present owners say they don't mind the odd happenings too much; Carmen is a nice enough ghost.

A most curious ghost is a tiny woman, barely four feet tall, known simply as the Ghost of Tubac (even though she never comes into the village proper). She strolls along the railroad tracks near the Circle Z Ranch, which was owned by the Proctor family. Many years ago, Gil Proctor's brother died within a few days of Gil seeing her, and around the same time, the earth swallowed up an old mesquite tree on the ranch, leaving a large hole.

The Proctors had several encounters with borderland ghosts. Late one night the family heard footsteps starting in the living room and ending in the kitchen by the wood range. The following night Gil's parents again heard footsteps. On the third night Gil's father, armed with flashlight and shotgun, prepared to catch a prowler.

They went through the house and checked all the locked doors, but they found no one. The next night their terrier barked and followed footsteps to a camouflaged wall. The footsteps belonged to the ghost of a man standing fourteen feet tall. He vanished, but a friend who lived with the family saw a beautiful glow near the site of the vanished mesquite tree. They never dared dig up the earth to see what secret was concealed there.

Five different flags—those of Spain, Mexico, the United States, the Confederacy, and the Arizona Territory—have flown over Tubac. Given the area's rich history, one could probably garner enough ghost stories for a book just by going from door to door and asking the owners, "Which ghost lives here?" Residents gladly answer the question, for they have made peace with their ghosts, and for the most part, enjoy talking about them.

Nick Bleser, a retired park ranger from Tumacacori, bought a Tubac house in 1984. The living room had served as the old mission store. Nick and his wife decided to remodel their house, and as is so often the case on making great changes to old buildings, they stirred up sleeping ghosts. The Blesers soon found that they were not alone. While Bleser was alone in the house, something threw a sock at the shower door. The sock had been missing for about two weeks. Now and again a young woman in the living room waits to be served by a clerk, and when no one comes, she gets disgusted and leaves. Occasionally a specter of an execution appears momentarily. Sometimes a dark, feminine hand turns out the lights. Today Bleser's wife sells Tubac real estate. She refuses to give her buyers a ghost guarantee.

Olga Leon's Tubac house must have a literary ghost, because her books simply drop off the shelves. In the house of Marjorie Nichols, children's ghosts have a good time—people have heard marbles rolling across the floor. Western artist Ross Stefan's studio and gallery are located in a former Chinese grocery, which was operated by Luis Lim from the turn of the century until 1929. Legend has it that Lim buried a fortune under the floors, and now ghosts frequent the building, likely searching for the treasure.

Long before Tubac was part of the United States, fortune hunters would hide their treasure maps in the houses of trusted friends. As years went by and people moved around, it was forgotten which houses held the maps. When one family moved into a Tubac house, they decided it was haunted because at night they saw a golden glow on one of the walls. Their neighbors decided the new people were *poco loco;* surely there must a hole in the roof letting in moon beams. They came over to check out the situation, and they saw the mysterious glow, too, but no hole in the roof.

The families decided to get together and tear down the wall. When they began digging underneath it, they found an underground room. Pieces of paper inside disintegrated upon exposure to air, and a hideous laugh echoed through the room. We can only suppose that they had forever lost maps that would have led them to valuable treasure. The ghost who guarded the maps was most pleased.

Strange lights have been seen in the sky between the Lewis and Seibold ranches near Patagonia. On the top of the highest hill near Washington Camp in Mowry, lights have often been seen from afar. At the ghost town of Alto you may look across a big arroyo and see a rock with the features of a Chinese man. Lights often flicker in the vicinity of this rock. Gabriel Montijo got curious and investigated them, and he died of a heart attack the next day.

During the 1700s, the Tohono O'odham, a peaceful tribe, mined silver around Alto. When it appeared that they might be attacked by

Apaches, the Tohono O'odhams stashed the silver nuggets back in the mine tunnel and sealed it. After several years, the old ones died and no one remembered just where the silver was hidden. In modern times, people have seen a ball of fire, brighter than any ordinary fire, rolling down the mountain around midnight, starting at the opening of an old Alto mine. Local residents stay far away from this fire. They claim that Native American spirits are sending the fire as signal to warn trespassers to stay away from the mine.

A headless horseman rides along the Arizona-Mexico border. He doesn't do anyone bodily harm, but he does make a general nuisance of himself by scaring decent people half witless. At night he stops people's cars and tells them to move over, and then he rides into the ditch and disappears. He'll walk through the front door of various ranch houses promptly at noon, jingling his spurs and looking in every room. If someone is in the room he says "Good afternoon" and leaves.

He particularly likes the Wiltshaw Ranch, nine miles south of Patagonia. Some say that one out of every family that lived at the Wiltshaw Ranch died a violent death. The headless horseman may be a former owner of the Wiltshaw who was killed in a car accident nearby. It is believed that he roams the desert looking for his head so he can cross over in peace—and in one piece.

Mountain caves hold ancient secrets. Perhaps it is best not to disturb them, but there are those who cannot resist the dark gaping void of a cavern. That was the case with three young men who went into the Onyx cave in the Santa Rita Mountains to explore, but never came out. Years later a couple of their friends tried to explore the cave. One of the spelunkers heard loud tapping and footsteps beneath him. He returned to the cave entrance, where his friend said he had been waiting for about two hours. Together they hunted for an opening in the floor of the cave, but they never found one. They concluded that the tapping was the sound of the spirits of the three dead explorers trying to find their way out.

Metal corrals now dot Arizona's ranching landscape, but once the fences were made of adobe. Back then, a vaquero working at a ranch near the Circle Z slept in an old adobe corral. He awoke in cold sweat and ran to the hacienda, where he awakened the family with a story that he had seen ghosts. They put him up in the barn for the rest of the night and investigated in the morning. Near the corral, they found a peculiar hole in the ground about the size of a child's grave.

Months later a man came up from Mexico and showed the family a treasure map. He claimed that his map showed that gold was buried near their corral, and he asked for permission to dig on their ranch. The family thought him a little loco but harmless, so they fed him and sent him on his way.

Still later a priest from Mexico came and asked if he could dig up a large rock in the center of the adobe corral. Now, priests exert a little more authority than vagrants do, and the husband was out somewhere, so the wife gave the holy man permission to go ahead and dig.

She had no idea that he intended to blast the rock to smithereens with dynamite—after all, it's just not the sort of thing priests do in the course of their duties. She heard a series of loud explosions, and by the time she got to the corral, the priest was riding off with a chest. What it contained, no one else knew.

Evidently he did not take the ghosts with him, for they are still seen near the ruins of the adobe corral on misty moonlit nights.

Early in the morning on December 25, 1944, when the Benitez family passed a house near Sahuarita, between Tucson and Nogales, they looked out the back window and saw a little girl standing in the doorway. The house was long abandoned and dark, and they could not imagine what a little girl might be doing there by herself. When they investigated, they found no one. Since then, many people have seen this childish ghost there on Christmas Eve.

Years ago Santos Gutierrez lived in a house in front of the El Rosario Cemetery in Nogales, Sonora. Her sister, who lived north of the border in Nogales, Arizona, was visiting Santos with her lovely new baby.

The first night of the visit at about midnight the baby woke up crying. The mother stood in the doorway of the house, holding and soothing the increasingly agitated child, when suddenly a priest with a lighted candle appeared, followed by a procession of wraith-like figures. The priest glanced at mother and child and walked on.

Santos's sister thought it was only a dream, but again the next night at midnight the baby cried. Again the priest led the procession past the door. This time the priest spoke to the mother, telling her that the only thing that saved her was the baby in her arms. "Tomorrow," he said, "I will take both you and your child." The baby slept through the next night, and when midnight came, the woman did not go to the door.

The occasional water in Apache Spring makes the site popular for camping. It is located near present-day Arivaca in Santa Cruz County and is also known as Apache Well. Should you camp there, you might wake during the night to find a shadowy, robed, monk-like figure standing over you.

The story has its beginnings when the United States took possession of southern Arizona. Many Mexican families decided to flee to Mexico, leaving their silver and gold with a trustworthy priest. The priest supposedly buried the treasures within view of Tumacacori. Over the years a number of the families returned from Mexico, and instead of retrieving their treasures, they agreed that the priest should only bring them out during feast days, weddings, and funerals.

One morning the old priest's housekeeper arrived to find him dead. After they had buried him, the families realized that no one knew where he had stashed their valuables. They searched everywhere, in every direction, but found nothing. Over the years cowboys, miners, and hikers who venture into this area have seen a priestly figure walking through the desert in the moonlight, but no one dares ask him about the treasure.

In Nogales, ghosts do not confine themselves to Roman Catholic churches. St. Andrew's Episcopal Church and its parsonage are built on a Native American burial ground. When a new rector arrived in 1976, he and his wife were awakened by a phantom figure of an old Native American man wrapped in a beautiful blanket standing at the foot of their bed. The old man appeared sad, but he had warm, kindly eyes and a gentle manner. They spoke to him, but he did not answer. Slowly he faded into the night, but he continued to appear from time to time. At first the rector tried exorcism, but it had no effect. The family decided to deal with the ghost with love. Once during a wedding, the ghost meandered through the church and grounds, mingling freely with the crowd.

If you happen to be crossing the Arizona-Mexico border around midnight in Nogales, a Mexican soldier from the days of Pancho Villa may stand at the twenty-one-kilometer point, motioning for you to stop. If you do, he will laugh a terrible, hellacious cackle. Should you find the courage to look into his eyes, you will get a glimpse of hell—and then you will find out what sort of person you truly are, for some who look into his eyes mend their ways here on earth, while others go mad and descend into hell.

If you're a serious ghost tracker, you might want to consider the devil tree—and then again, you might not. The devil tree, hidden in secluded woods off of Pennington Road near Nogales, features an upside-down cross burned on its trunk. On your way into the woods to find it, you may meet a creature with the body of a dog and the face of a man. If he sees you, he will bare his fangs and growl an unearthly sound. Hurry on, before he does worse.

Should you find the Devil Tree on the night of a full moon, you are sure to witness a most evil, eerie ceremony of phantom devils. The place will smell of sulfur, and shadowy forms will open their gaping mouths to scream ungodly, largely unintelligible screams that escalate from the depths of hell—but if you listen closely, you may make out the words "We are legion."

chapter 2

Quest for the Soul

Why if the Soul can fling the dust aside,
And naked on the air of Heaven ride
Weren't not a shame—weren't not a shame for him
In this clay carcasse crippled to abide?
                    —Omar Khayyam, *The Rubaiyat*

For Arizonans, November 1949 provided many more important matters for discussion than the disappearance of a vagrant miner who believed in spirits. Harry S. Truman had pulled off a surprise victory over Thomas E. Dewey in the presidential election and a young Arizona politician, Barry M. Goldwater, was just beginning to make his mark.

The missing prospector, James Kidd, was seventy years old in November 1949 and living on the edge of poverty in Phoenix. He often worked out his rent by doing odd jobs and yard work for his landlord. On the night of November 9, Kidd visited an acquaintance, David Crumrine, who lived nearby. After holding a brief, cordial conversation and borrowing a prospector's pick, Kidd set out for home on foot. Along the way he met Pete Eastman and chatted briefly with him.

Eastman and Crumrine could hardly be called Kidd's friends; they didn't know him very well and had never questioned him about his past. Kidd told each of them that he would be leaving the next morning with a friend who owned a car to work his claims, but he did not give the friend's name.

The next morning, neighbors heard a car screeching to a stop and a door slamming shut at 335 North Ninth Avenue, where Kidd lived. Kidd left and never returned.

None of his neighbors thought it unusual for Kidd to be gone for several days. However, when he did not return by December 29, his landlord, F. J. Pentowski, reported him missing to the Phoenix Police. After inspecting Kidd's one-room apartment, Phoenix Police Officer William Gragg determined that Kidd had expected to return soon.

Kidd's rent was just four dollars a week. He never owned a car or possessed a driver's license; he got around by walking, taking the bus, or hitchhiking. In restaurants he always ordered the cheapest meal on the menu and kept an eye out for a newspaper left behind. He made a nickel cigar last all day. Yet Officer Gragg found among Kidd's personal possessions, paperwork indicating that he had $3,800 in a Valley National Bank checking account and had recently received a dividend check from the Hudson Bay Mines and Smelting Company in the amount of $382. A suitcase uncovered additional financial records. For awhile people speculated that Kidd might have been murdered and shoved down one of Arizona's many open mine shafts in some place like Graveyard Canyon or Bloody Tanks Wash. Because Kidd had no heirs and as yet, not much of an estate, no one made much effort to find him.

Kidd might have been forgotten if not for three things: a 1956 Arizona law about distributing unclaimed property, the huge fortune it turned out Kidd had accumulated, and a bizarre clause in his will, which wouldn't be found until he'd been missing more than twenty years. The will stated that Kidd's money should be used to research the existence of the human soul.

Kidd arrived in Miami, Arizona, around 1920. On his voter registration he stated that he was born in Ogdensburg, New York, on July 18, 1879. While employed at the Miami Copper Mining Company, Kidd regulated the pumps that carried the tailings away from the mine. His pay would have been about five dollars a day during the 1920s and 1930s.

In 1933, Kidd registered two mining claims, Scorpion 1 and Scorpion 2. For fifteen years he kept up the affidavits of labor and made his yearly payments at the Gila County Recorder's Office to keep his claims active. Some people think the claims are in the Pinto Creek area, while others believe that they may be located in the Superstition Mountains. Kidd's descriptions for Scorpion 1 and Scorpion 2, as recorded in Gila County records, are the same for both claims:

> Lode Claim To Whom it may Concern: This mining claim of which is Scorpion #1 situated on lands belonging to the U. S. A. and in which there are valuable deposits was entered upon and located for the purpose of exploration and purchase by Walter H. Beach and James Kidd, citizens. The length of this claim is 1,500 long feet and 600 feet wide in an easterly direction. This claim is situated and located in the Miami Mining District in Gila County.

The claims have never been found. Kidd's partner, Walter H. Beach, died two years before Kidd disappeared.

Staring out of his only photograph, Kidd is an attractive, well-dressed middle-aged man with a slightly cynical smile. According to Kidd's coworkers at the Miami Copper Mining Company, he never discussed money. He never drank and rarely gambled. Although he was unmarried, he had an eye for pretty women. He was remembered as a quiet, pale man who had an eastern accent and quoted Omar Khayyam. At night he liked to talk about the supernatural, musing about what was out there.

Kidd was bald and never removed his charcoal-gray fedora. In fact, in September 1942, he collapsed in a pumping station accident, and when nurses at the Miami-Inspiration Hospital asked him to remove his hat, he became enraged.

Kidd filed for workman's compensation as a result of the pump accident. The state disallowed the claim on the basis that his heart problem, not the accident, had incapacitated him. He refused a position as mine watchman and moved to the one-room hovel in Phoenix.

After Kidd disappeared, Phoenix police, unable to find him, passed on their information to the Federal Bureau of Investigation (FBI) and the Globe-Miami police. While working for the Miami Copper Company, Kidd stayed at cheap rooming houses and always received his mail at General Delivery. His personal papers revealed that he had previously lived in Reno and Los Angeles. Pat Nathan, a stockbroker with E. F. Hutton Company, saw Kidd on a regular basis, but he said that Kidd never divulged information about relatives or close friends. "Suddenly Kidd just went out of my life," Nathan said.

In 1956, the Arizona Legislature passed the Uniform Disposition of Unclaimed Property Act. This law, a monument to bureaucratic paperwork, stipulated that property unclaimed after seven years should revert to the state of Arizona. Geraldine Swift, Arizona estate tax commissioner, became a receiving agent for thousands of accounts, including those of James Kidd.

E. F. Hutton sent Swift its report on the Kidd account, along with a check for $18,000 from liquidated securities. At the Bank of Douglas in Douglas, Arizona, two trust officers drilled Kidd's safe deposit box open and found additional stock and copies of Kidd's photograph. Records indicated that Kidd had acquired thousands of shares of stock during the 1920s and 1930s. When reports were completed, the Kidd estate totaled almost $300,000 in cash and stocks found mostly in safe deposit boxes in Phoenix and Los Angeles.

Records also indicated that on April 16, 1950, six months after Kidd disappeared, someone using Kidd's name accessed his safe deposit box in the Bank of Douglas. The signed entry slip appeared to be in Kidd's handwriting. Did he—or his ghost—remove securities or add more stocks? Did someone, possibly his murderer, commit an excellent case of forgery? If the signed slip was forged, then how did the forger come to possess the requisite key to the safe deposit box?

Every year as part of her duties implementing the Uniform Disposition of Unclaimed Property Act, Geraldine Swift checked the accounts that had not been closed in the catacombs of the Valley National Bank in Phoenix. Over the years she became attached to the Kidd account. Perhaps she felt a twinge of sadness when she looked at the picture of the man nobody missed.

On January 11, 1964, while Swift flipped through a sheath of Kidd's stock purchase receipts, a handwritten note fell out. Swift was stunned when she realized that she had discovered James Kidd's will. It stated:

This is my first and only will and is dated the second of January 1946. I have no heirs and have not been married in my life and after all my funeral expenses have been paid and about $100, one hundred dollars to some preacher of the gospital [sic] to say farewell at my grave sell all my property which is all in cash and stocks with E. F. Hutton Co. In Phoenix some is in safety box, and have this balance money to go in a reserach [sic] or some scientific proof of a soul of the human body which leaves at death. I think in time their [sic] can be a photograph of the soul leaving the human at death,

James Kidd

Swift showed her findings to her assistant and an Arizona state tax auditor, who said alternately, "Tsk, Tsk!" and "I'll be damned!" They compared Kidd's signature on his safe deposit card and the will and found that they matched.

The Arizona attorney general's staff was considerably divided on what should be done with Kidd's will. Assistant Attorney General Robert Murless suggested that Swift destroy it so that the considerable sum of money would revert to the state of Arizona, but Swift insisted that the will should be probated in accordance with Kidd's wishes. She filed a routine petition for probate by the state of Arizona.

The petition went to Judge Robert L. Myers of the Superior Court of Maricopa County. Questions immediately arose. What did Kidd mean by "research or some scientific proof"? Did an applicant for the monies have to prove that a soul left the body? How would the court record nonstandard testimony like witnesses employing extrasensory perception? How could the judge determine which individual or institution should receive the money?

Even before the judge's opinion could be announced, the University of Life Church filed a motion to dismiss the state's petition to take over Kidd's estate. The church, under the Reverend. Richard T. Ireland, saw itself as unequivocally qualified to prove life after death because it conducted seances and had frequent communication with those beyond the grave. Ireland, an unordained minister, combined his extrasensory perception abilities with hell-and-brimstone preaching.

On May 6, 1965, Judge Myers announced that the will would be probated. One hundred thirty-three claimants paid the fifteen-dollar fee to file a claim on Kidd's money, and over a thousand inquiries came from all over the United States and the world. Judge Myers added stamps from Thailand, India, Germany, France, South America, and Canada to his collection. Hearings began on June 6, 1967.

Vagrant miner James Kidd, whom no one cared enough about to look for when he disappeared, acquired a host of devoted brothers, wives, and children. Maxine Tustian of Toronto said she was Kidd's niece, and two women claimed that they had been married to Kidd and that he deserted them, though neither woman would explain why she had never searched for him.

One of the "wives" claimed that she married Kidd in 1913. She would never attempt to get the money for herself, the Wisconsin woman said, but she might petition for their two darling daughters.

While working as a waitress in Flagstaff, Arizona, Elyse Demontmollin Kidd, originally from New York, got the good news that she was going to be a wealthy woman. She claimed that she and Kidd were married in Baja California, Mexico, in December 1937. Her story was that Kidd deserted her in Los Angeles after two years of marriage and she never heard from him again. Her memory was very hazy on the two years they were supposed to have been married. Elyse produced a photocopy of a phony Mexican marriage license that she said had been validated by the American consulate in Mexico. Myers disallowed her petition when Miami Copper Company officials provided documents that Kidd was working for them on the day he was supposedly married in Mexico. A handwriting expert testified that Kidd's signature on the Mexican marriage certificate was forged.

Two men from Ontario, eighty-one-year-old John Herbert Kidd and eighty-three-year-old Herman Silas Kidd, claimed to be blood brothers of the deceased (or, more correctly, "the disappeared"). The Kidd brothers contended that the will proved James Kidd was not of sound mind, and his estate should be shared with his heirs. Both men died before the hearing was over.

Institutions hitherto indifferent to the afterlife now presented themselves as devout spiritual believers. The University of Arizona Board of Regents, represented by Gary Nelson, first made application on behalf of the proposed University of Arizona College of Medicine, which was still in the planning stages and ten years from being built. When the regents saw that their premise probably could not win, Northern Arizona University went for the big bucks. NAU wanted the money for a James Kidd Chair in its philosophy department.

The Neurological Sciences Foundation of Phoenix, through the Barrow Neurological Institute at the local St. Joseph's Hospital, presented its qualifications by citing its painstaking work on the labyrinthine nervous system of cats. The alleged Kidd heirs wanted to know if the institute believed that cats had souls. The Barrow Foundation's counsel responded that the nervous system of the cat was similar to that of a human.

Single petitioners got the attention of the court in an unorthodox fashion. A man from Kansas wrote, "I am not a soul. I do not belong to any human group on earth." Attorney Paul Sloane, who filed for himself, contended that the money should be divided among various universities, with himself as co-trustee. Lieutenant Colonel Virat Ambudha received a leave of absence from the Thai army to make his claim on Kidd's fortune. Phoenix steelworker Leroy Branham said that an hour after his father died, his father's spirit told him that he had been poisoned for his money. If the judge would only order his father's body exhumed, Branham would prove that he was the best to receive the money. Probably one of the most honest petitioners was a woman who just wanted some of Kidd's loot to buy herself a new pair of false teeth.

A deluge of soul seekers—philosophers, spiritualists, psychics, swamis, yogis, clairvoyants, and deluded lunatics—claimed Kidd's money. All were willing to make themselves look downright silly by arguing that they were the best suited to prove the existence of the soul.

The Reverend Robert Raleigh, bishop of the Church of Antioch, told the court that his blindness had opened his spiritual eyes to the riddle of the human soul. He claimed that his church was founded by the Apostle Peter in A.D. 38. After Judge Myers disallowed his petition, Raleigh insisted that only God could make the decision in this case and that Myers had no right to usurp the power of God.

One woman who called herself the Holy Spirit Virgin said she was living proof of the existence of a soul. Ludwig Rosecrans, a longtime hermit from the Superstition Mountains, claimed that he had faced a "most unusual and horrifying experience" in which it was revealed to him that the world had a nervous breakdown with the explosion of the atomic bomb. He described this in a manuscript called *The Kingdom of Reality*, which he wanted to publish using Kidd's money. James E. Rea, assistant professor of philosophy at Northern Arizona University, insisted that when someone dies, multicolored globs the size of silver dollars, visible to the human eye, leave the earthly body.

Two housewives who were in touch with the spirits flew their earthly bodies in from California. Nora Higgins, vocal and challenging, insisted that Kidd was in the courtroom and had whispered to her that "things were not working out." That could be made right, of course, by awarding her the money. Jean Bright from Encino said that she was in constant communication with her deceased dentist, who would help her prove the existence of a soul. She used earplugs and a noisy hair dryer to prove her point. The judge, being rather undiscerning, would not permit voices from beyond to be entered into testimony.

Earl Johnson, a transient with a long white beard, said he was born dead but came to life a little later, and if the judge did not believe his story, then that was his problem. Having spent two weeks in a Missouri insane asylum, Johnson produced a certificate to prove that he was sane.

Sometime during the hearings, a letter from James Kidd arrived on Judge Myers's desk. The plain white envelope had no return address and was postmarked Phoenix. It contained a missive that read:

If you are wondering why this letter is typed, 8 years ago I was hurt in a fall and my hand is partially paralyzed. My handwriting is now illegible. I have a false name and I am watching this whole thing about the distribution of my money. I have always wanted to see what a person would do if given the chance to get a large amount of money. Please go on and find a worthy person for my money. Thank you for your concern. Quite alive,

James Kidd

All told, the hearings went on for thirteen weeks of legal legerdemain and psychic science. Because this was a hearing and not a trial, everyone could question everyone else, and they did. Lawyers tediously and painstaking presented their cases. Philosophers wallowed in Jung and Freud. Everybody struggled with legalistic soul searching.

On September 1, 1967, the hearings of Probate Case Number 58416 in the matter of James Kidd, deceased, came to an end. All heir aspirant claims were thrown out for lack of substantiation. On October 20, Myers awarded the money to the Barrow Neurological Institute in Phoenix.

The Kidd case did not end with Myers's ruling, for on January 19, 1971, the Arizona Supreme Court overthrew it and sent the case back to court. The justices overturned the case on the basis that Barrow had never done, and did not intend to do, research on the human soul.

The Arizona Supreme Court instructed Myers to give the money to one of four claimants who had done previous soul research: the American Society for Psychical Research, the Psychical Research Foundation, Dr. Joseph Still of Los Angeles, or Reverend Russell Dilts of South Bend, Indiana.

Still, represented by the well-known criminal lawyer, Melvin Belli, was a practicing physician who had written a book, *Cybernetic Theory of Aging.* He theorized that there were three types of death and life, and that a soul was associated with psychic death and life.

Dilts, from South Bend, Indiana, described himself as an investigator of departed spirits. In court he produced a photo that he claimed was Kidd's soul. It showed Dilts seated in a chair with an outline of Kidd's face looking over his shoulder.

Ultimately the money went to the Psychical Research Association and the American Society for Psychical Research, Inc. Under these organizations, Kidd's estate funded studies on the auras of dying persons. Karlis Osis and Erlendur Haraldsson published their findings in a book called *At the Hour of Death.* The results were also published in the *Journal of the American Society for Psychical Research.* A soul or a ghost leaving the body has not yet been captured on film, but at least Kidd's fortune went for work that he wanted to fund.

Mysteries still remain unsolved. What happened to James Kidd? How did he amass such a fortune? As we shall see, he was not the only Arizonan who believed that mortals are able to see the spirit after it leaves the body.

chapter 3

Phantoms of the Desert

If you believe inanimate objects have no soul, you've likely never heard the peal of the golden bell of San Marcelo de Sonoyta. You've probably never jumped out of the way of a phantom train as it chugged across the Willcox Playa, either, and odds are you haven't seen the sails of a pirate galleon rise out of the Yuma desert. If you *had* seen these marvels, you might well believe that everything has a spirit. Yes, you might well believe that.

Often we hear stories and wonder where they came from. These stories started on the Arizona desert, long ago but not too far away.

The story of the golden bell begins in the 1700s, when a great Jesuit missionary, Padre Eusebio Kino, established a *visita*, or chapel, at the town of Sonoyta along the present U.S.-Mexico border. This mission prospered until one particular priest arrived. Every time this priest rang the bell, an earthquake shook the land. (Lest, gentle reader, you should think an earthquake impossible in Arizona, an 1887 earthquake was estimated to measure seven on the Richter scale, and it destroyed much of southern Arizona and northern Mexico.)

25

To rid their land of this evil, the Tohono O'odham people (formerly known as the Papago Indians) felt they had no choice but to kill the priest. That done, they wrapped the bell in a blanket and buried it in a cave near Quitobaquito, but even the earth could not muffle the sound of it. The Tohono O'odhams soon realized their mistake when they discovered that the padre was not at fault: The bell didn't cause earthquakes, it only warned when earthquakes were about to happen. Even buried in the ground, the bell rang whenever an earthquake shook the land.

Around 1932, puzzling reports circulated around southern Arizona concerning a solid gold bell with a beautiful tone that had been found at an unspecified mission somewhere on the Tohono O'odham Reservation. Not everybody thought the bell sounded beautiful; certain unkind souls contended that it sounded slightly lower in pitch than a Southern Pacific locomotive, while other nonbelievers compared it to a Brahma bull in the throes of passion.

Some have postulated that the golden bell may not have been golden at all but might have its name borrowed from the hymn "When They Ring the Golden Bells for You and Me," which is a part of many church repertoires. This is unlikely because this Protestant Pentecostal song is more suited to skid row rescue missions than Spanish Catholic mission churches. The bell was probably created at the Altar Valley brass foundry in Sonora and would have used local ores including copper, lead, galena, silver, and gold. It was likely constructed of a metal alloy, and if molds were not available it would have been of imperfect design with a slightly sour tone. Sweet or sour, the golden bell served a good purpose by warning people of an impending earthquake.

After World War II, an ancient bell went on display at Wellton, a small farming community near Yuma. It was purportedly the bell of San Marcelo Sonoitac (an old spelling of the Mexican town Sonoyta), though it now belonged to Hugh Spain, who ran a Wellton tourist camp. According to Spain's wife, Madelaine, in an interview in the 1970s, the bell was cast circa 1604 of a very soft yellow metal. It stood thirteen inches in height, measured eighteen inches at its greatest diameter, and weighed about sixty pounds. Madelaine described how the San Marcelo priests removed it from the chapel during the Pima revolt of 1770, when members of the Pima tribe destroyed the mission and killed Father Enrique Rhuen. She said the golden bell, which had a chipped crown and missing clapper and clapper linkage, was given to her husband by Isobel Parra, who in turn had obtained it from the Tohono O'odhams at Santa Margarita, a village south of Sells, Arizona.

You might think this would end the mystery of the golden bell. Not so.

Mrs. Spain claimed that her husband's bell was destroyed at the tourist camp in 1943—yet to this day there are still those in the area who hear a bell chiming whenever the earth begins to quake.

Near Willcox, Arizona, between the Dragoon and Little Dragoon mountain ranges, rests a dry, shallow, prehistoric lake bed, the Willcox Playa. This barren piece of flat alkaline soil has been variously called the Playas, Soda Lake, Dry Lake, and Alkali Flats. It is a somber, forbidding place. Nothing lives there—nothing but mirages.

Scientists tell us mirages are simply optical phenomena created by layers of hot air of varying density that bend or reflect light. Nonetheless, the intense, brilliant mirages of the Sonoran desert that appear as pools of water or reflections of far-off objects can be quite disturbing.

Mirages on the Playas usually involve an astonishing expanse of cool blue water spread across the dry desert. During World War II, two navy pilots ferrying a boat across the country thought they saw the Atlantic Ocean, or some other such large body of water, as they flew over the Playas. The navy pilots made a bumpy unauthorized landing on the dry lake bed. When they discovered that they were in Arizona, the embarrassed pilots had a lot of explaining to do.

There also exists an entirely different sort of Playas mirage. No matter that the nearest train siding is on the far side of the mountains; in the Playas, if you listen carefully, you might hear the whistle of a steam engine and the clatter of wheels, and at night, a blinding engine light bears down on you.

Few would want to climb aboard the phantom train of the Playas, and certainly not lean, handsome young Billy Barclay. Barclay, late of Iowa, didn't fit in with the ragtag population of 1870s Tombstone, Arizona. Prospectors, pimps, rotten row lawyers, hurdy-gurdy girls, and associated scoundrels lived in Tombstone, and those in training as desperadoes flourished. Billy was different. He bathed whenever he could find water. He did not imbibe strong spirits, shoot people, cuss, gamble, chase other men's wives, or consort with the soiled doves of Allen Street. He didn't even go to church. In short, Billy Barclay was a Tombstone eccentric, tolerated because he minded his own business.

Billy became heartily tired of cheap boardinghouses. He had been given a room in Tombstone and was told that he would not find its equal in all of Arizona. He agreed with that part, though he didn't find the superlatives to be of the positive sort. The building was constructed of one-inch lumber with a canvas roof. Rooms were divided by cheesecloth nailed to scantlings. A whisper at one end easily could be heard at the other. In the summer the building was hotter than a Turkish bath and acted as vacation resort to scorpions. On Sundays the proprietor served his boarders wine thick as crude oil and strong as chloroform.

After a few years of virtuous living, Billy discovered that he had nothing more than his room in the cheap boardinghouse, a hundred dollars in gold, a rifle and pistol for hunting, and a respectable handlebar moustache on his handsome, chiseled face. To make matters worse, Billy felt strange flutterings in his chest when Jenny Martin, the new Tombstone schoolmarm, rustled her skirts and smiled shyly under the large brim of her Sunday hat.

Jenny lived as virtuously as Billy did, and more so, for she took in the elegant drama productions at Schiefflin Hall and attended services at Reverend Endicott Peabody's Episcopal church. Jenny also sipped tea at the rectory and appeared at the good preacher's lectures on the Life of St. Paul. Never did she turn down Allen Street to the Bird Cage Theater, where she might be mistaken for Big Nose Kate, Mollie the Gold Digger, Crazy Horse Lil, or Dutch Annie.

Billy felt certain that Jenny liked him. It became increasingly clear that the only wasp in the honey was his impoverished state. And although several Tombstone mines closed in 1879, rumors spread of a mother lode of gold near Dos Cabezas.

To say that July summers in southern Arizona are hot is a little like saying that the Sears Tower is a tall building. The temperature hovered around 110 degrees over the sixty miles of open desert that Billy had to cross to reach his destination. The path was lined with cactus, rattlesnakes, poisonous lizards, and vicious bugs—but like all who heed the call of El Dorado, Billy felt a sense of urgency.

Billy lightly loaded his burro, Nellie, with only the necessities and filled his canvas canteen with water. Squinting in the direction of Dos Cabezas, Billy mopped his brow with his kerchief and pulled the brim of his white Stetson over his eyes. He had only one question: Should he go around or cross the Playas? He opted for crossing. No use in losing a whole day to go around. And so Billy left Tombstone, cautious but confident.

That evening he shared his water, hard tack, and jerky with Nellie. He also made his first mistake: He did not picket his burro when he bedded down. Why would he? In the years and hundreds of miles they had covered together, the trustworthy little jenny had never wandered off. Billy made a pillow of his pack and fell asleep under a creosote bush with Nellie standing nearby.

A hideous, inhuman scream woke Billy up. When he came to his senses he realized that the scream had come from a cougar making a kill. Billy saw the cat finishing off his burro in the moonlight. He raised his rifle, but it was too late. The cougar disappeared into the darkness.

Billy wept over the butchered carcass of his beloved Nellie, but he did not have time to waste on heartache. In her efforts to escape, Nellie had tromped through his food, cutting his water jug with her sharp hooves. Very little water remained. It would have been sensible to return to Tombstone, but gold seekers rarely operate with a full deck. Billy started out for Dos Cabezas on foot, finding his way by the stars.

By mid-morning the sun was relentless. No tree offered him shade or succor. He drank the last of his water and tossed the flask aside. Before long, his tongue began to swell, and he recognized the early symptoms of cottonmouth.

Never was Billy so happy to see a barrel cactus. He pulled his knife out of his boot and slashed through its heavy, hooked spines, removed the cactus top, yanked out a chunk of the pulp, and sucked out the bitter liquid. Nausea gripped his belly. The cactus was all he had; without it, he would surely die.

Knowing that barrel cacti, also known as compass cacti, always lean southward, Billy oriented himself and slowly trudged onwards. The cactus juice eased his thirst, and he sensed a resurgence of strength.

Billy was overjoyed when he saw a blue lake. He kept walking towards it, anticipating the cool, refreshing water, but he never reached it. Finally he saw footsteps ahead of him. After awhile he placed his feet in the footprints and realized they were his own. He had been walking in circles. The cool water was a mirage.

Billy sobbed over the futility of his situation. Then he heard the chug of a train engine. A train engine! Billy stared at the oncoming locomotive, but he saw no tracks. Having had enough of cruel deceit, Billy refused to believe his eyes.

The image grew sharper. Smoke belched from the stack and bells warned anything that stood in the train's path. The train bore down on him, and instinct told him to get out of the way before he was crushed, but Billy stood as if riveted to the ground. The train stopped just inches from him, the engineer calling, "All aboard!"

Billy stood dazed. The engineer pulled out his watch and said, "Hurry! We're late!" When Billy did not move, the conductor and the brakeman yanked him up the steps and into a passenger car. The engine hissed and sputtered as it stirred into motion. A heavy door closed behind him.

Curious but kind faces stared down at Billy through a misty haze. They shook their heads. "Poor fellow. He is really bad off. Do you think he'll make it?"

Billy uttered one word through cracked lips: "Water." The conductor brought him a cool cup. Billy drank greedily before sinking into a deep sleep.

The next morning Billy Barclay woke up in the sheriff's office in Willcox. A man by the name of Crowley had found him walking in circles near the Playas. Several people in the office listened when the deputy asked Billy who he was and where he came from. Billy told them about the burro and the train. They nodded sympathetically, but he could see in their eyes that they did not believe him.

Billy asked, "What day is it?"

When they told him, he learned the reason for their disbelief. They had found him on the morning of the day he left Tombstone. He could never have walked over sixty miles through the desert in that short span of time. Billy repeated his story about the train.

They looked knowingly at each other and said he must have gotten his dates mixed up. The sun had scrambled his brain. No train ever crossed the Playas. But Billy Barclay knew what he had seen, and it would never do to say otherwise. For the rest of his life he wondered: Where did that train come from? Who were those people who ministered to him on the Playas?

The walking sands of the Yuma Desert and Mexico's Gran Desierto have a way of uncovering treasures—perhaps a golden bell, perhaps a lost pirate ship—and then shifting to cover them again as soon as a treasure hunter returns to the site with friends. Having endured the hoots and sniggers of bar cronies, many might be inclined to dismiss such treasures as mirages.

However, the story of a lost British pirate ship "sailing" on dry desert is true—parts of it, anyway. It begins on July 31, 1586, when Captain Thomas Cavendish sailed from Plymouth, England, with his three barkentines: the *Hugh Gallant*, the *Content*, and the *Desire*. He carried letters of marque from Queen Elizabeth I mandating him to plunder and demolish Spanish ships.

Cavendish traveled down the coast of Africa through the Straits of Magellan and to the coast of Ecuador. When scurvy and desertion took a toll on his crew, he scuttled the *Hugh Gallant* so that he would have enough men for the crews of the *Content* and the *Desire*. Cavendish's crews raided the coastal towns of Chile and Peru but got very little in the way of riches for their efforts.

On July 19, 1587, Cavendish defeated a Spanish ship off the coast of El Salvador. The ship was in ballast and carried little of value. However, the English captured a French pilot who went by the alias of Miguel Sanchez. After a proper amount of time and torture, Sanchez revealed that two Spanish galleons from Manila were due to put into port at Acapulco, Mexico. Cavendish, knowing these ships would carry prize booty, sailed northward.

A month later, Cavendish's ships patrolled the Acapulco waters, waiting and watching for their quarry. The Spanish galleon *Santa Ana*, five weeks out of Manila, entered Acapulco waters on November 14. Captain Tomas de Alzola scanned the horizon and saw the sails of the *Desire* and the *Content*. At first, he took them to be Spanish pearlers headed for Mazatlan, but the next morning he saw that they were enemy pirate ships closing in on him.

The *Desire* opened fire with a cannon barrage and sailed alongside the *Santa Ana*. Cavendish boarded the Spanish ship with a party of forty men. Facing the English ship's overwhelming weapons and manpower, Alzola's crew had no choice but to surrender.

The *Desire* and the *Content* towed their quarry into San Lucas Bay in the Gulf of California. Here the English put their prisoners ashore, equipping them with limited supplies and sails for tents. Cavendish took stock of his booty, which consisted of Chinese carvings, silks, perfumes, religious statues, chinaware, and provisions. To his delight, Cavendish also discovered a strongbox containing over one hundred thousand pesos in gold and a cache of fine pearls. His crews argued about the division of the spoils, but Cavendish insisted on dividing it into three parts: one for the queen, one for himself, and one for the crew. This appeared to satisfy everyone, but appearances never tell the whole story.

On November 19, the English pirates sailed out of San Lucas Bay after firing a final salvo and sinking the *Santa Ana*. The *Content* followed the *Desire* into the Gulf, each ship carrying half the treasure. Then the *Content* began to lag farther and farther behind.

The *Desire* arrived in Plymouth, England, on September 20, 1588, with its portion of the treasure intact. Queen Elizabeth promptly knighted Cavendish. No such happy fortune awaited the *Content*. The ship never arrived in England and its crew was never heard from again.

Speculation is that the crew of the *Content* mutinied and threw the officers overboard when the ship left San Lucas Bay. If this speculation is true, and if Cavendish had caught the crew, they would surely have hanged once they got back to England.

The crew didn't hang, but their fate may have been worse. Because maps of those days showed Baja California as an island rather than the long peninsula that it is, the *Content* crew likely would have decided to sail in the opposite direction of the *Desire*, only to find themselves at a dead end. The ship could have marooned on a wicked lava reef, only to be pushed ashore on a tidal wave. After depleting their food and liquor, the mutineers most certainly perished in the desert. Over the centuries, desert sands filled in the shoreline and covered the pirate galleon.

The shifting sands of the desert decide when and where to reveal its treasures. If you are in the right place, the winds are blowing in the right direction, and the sands are walking, you might see the *Content* hoist her sails in the desert. You will have to hurry to find her, for she is a restless ghost. But if you do, try to get her to reveal her secret horde of gold and pearls.

Got to go now! I hear a bell ringing, and my train is coming down the track. And would you just look at that sailing ship on the horizon?

chapter 4

On the Road Again

Arizona's fiendish freeways have always attracted evil, and I don't just mean road rage at California drivers. This is especially so on Route 666—the Highway to Hell, Satan's Speedway, the Devil's Dragstrip—which used to cover a two-hundred-mile stretch of haunted asphalt in Arizona, Colorado, and New Mexico. The bizarre events along this road definitely make it the road less traveled.

The only place you can still get your kicks on the real honest-to-goodness 666 is in Colorado; Arizona and New Mexico have changed the name of their portion of the road. When the Arizona Department of Transportation changed the state's portion of 666 to 191 in November 1992, the official story was that they were conforming to the national system of assigning odd numbers to north-south routes—the change had nothing to do with religion (or lack of it). And though the name change may have stopped those with ungodly motives from stealing the road signs, many Arizonans contend that it didn't do anything to dispel the highway's aura of evil.

Revelation 13:8 says, "Let him who has understanding calculate the number of the beast, for it is the number of a man: His number is 666."

Satan and all his minions are believed to have the number 666 emblazoned somewhere on their bodies. Some people believe this means that Route 666 is nothing less than Satan's zip code, discounting the evidence that the road's many fatalities are caused by drunks, accidents, and poor driving conditions.

No matter what you believe about the highway and no matter what you call it, don't look into your rear-view mirror when you drive it—what you see would strike terror in the hearts of the brave. The most common grotesque specters along the highway include Satan, a deranged truck driver, a flock of eerie birds, a pack of mad dogs, a faceless giant, and a vanishing hitchhiker, all intent on mayhem.

Although Satan sometimes brazenly saunters along the road during the day, he more often appears on full-moon nights driving Satan's Sedan, a vehicle of unknown make and model. He plays chicken with motorists, driving at them head-on, often causing them to swerve off the road and down a cliff. He's also been known to haunt the roadside, a spectral horned figure dressed in red tights, using a pitchfork to puncture tourists' car tires. Drivers make the repairs with dispatch, only to have the tires blow out again a few hundred feet down the road.

The demented trucker loves to crush pedestrians beneath his blood-red rig. Stranded motorists who have had their tires punctured by the devil often try to flag down the truck driver, only to find themselves plastered against the rig's radiator.

Others have seen a flock of white birds flying in a V formation over the hoods of vehicles, keeping pace with cars at speeds from twenty to one hundred miles per hour. Even more vexatious are the savage packs of devil dogs. The hounds attack cars and tear their tires to shreds. When the cars pull over, the bloodthirsty curs break through the windows and rip up the screaming passengers.

Motorists cruising along 666 at night have sensed that danger is near when they cut into a carrot purchased at a roadside stop a few miles back and discover remnants of bones. They catch an image in their rear-view mirror, human shaped but without human features, about nine feet tall and reeking of burning sulfur. The rear window implodes into the vehicle at the same time the radio starts playing Charlie Daniels's "The Devil Went

Down to Georgia." Afterwards, the motorists find no projectile such as a bullet or a rock to explain the broken window.

Not everyone agrees with changing the name of Route 666. After all, if 666 is the devil's address, where will he go when there is no 666? He will have to move—maybe to your street. Then your property values will go straight to hell.

With roads come cars and glorious opportunity for teenagers to get away from the tedium of studying and parents' watchful eyes. Parents tell their teens frightening stories to keep them from finding love nests in secluded spots on country roads, but we all know how futile that tactic can be. The young will always find love nests when they feel the need, and in Arizona, a ghostly killer named Hook will likely find them there. When Hook is present and a couple is particularly amorous, a white mist comes over their car (or at least that's what lovers say about steamy windows). And then, mysteriously, the car refuses to start. Hook has his young victims right where he wants them.

I am quite comfortable telling you this story because it was told to me by Maude Davis, a truthful woman who can personally vouch for the story's veracity. Maude's story starts with a series of emergency bulletins that came over Arizona radio some years back:

> Please watch out for a murderer who has escaped from the Arizona Insane Asylum at 24th and Van Buren in Phoenix. He attacks teenagers parking at night in remote places. He is about six foot three, two hundred pounds, with black hair. This homicidal maniac has a hook on one arm in place of a hand and he likes to use it to rip open his victims' bodies.

What the police could not say without looking perfectly silly is that the maniac pestering the city was the ghost of Hook, a man who, while still alive, liked to spy on young lovers. His hand was replaced with a hook after it was slammed in a car door by a couple who caught him watching. Hook was murdered years before by a lumberjack from the sawmill at the top of

Dead Man's Curve near Williams, Arizona—but in death, as in life, he loved to play peeping Tom.

The way Maude tells the story is that after the prom, she and her boyfriend were parked out on Camelback Road when they got the creepy feeling that they were being watched as they smooched. They heard a strange scratching on the roof and took off for home. When they got to Maude's house, Maude's boyfriend walked her to her front door. After they finished their kisses and hugs, he told her goodnight and walked back to the car. Something on the door handle, shining in the moonlight, caught his eye. It was a hook with dangling leather straps. Blood dripped from it down the side of the car.

Others have not been so fortunate in their all-too-close encounters with Mr. Hook. A few nights after Maude's encounter, another couple parked in a secluded woodland area. They had been to a dance and had dined on a big meal at a fancy restaurant. As they listened to the radio, the emergency bulletin aired again. When the boy turned on the ignition, the car would not start.

He said, "Connie, you wait here. We must be out of gas. I'm going to the service station just a few blocks down the road. Lock the doors as soon as I get out and don't let anyone come in. I'll be right back." Connie agreed, asking him to hurry.

Pretty soon she heard an unholy ruckus outside, and then an insistent scratching on the roof. It sounded like someone scraping fingernails across a blackboard. After awhile the tapping stopped, but her boyfriend didn't come back. Minutes turned into hours, and Connie turned on the radio to keep herself awake. It was no use. She couldn't keep her eyes open.

She awoke when a policeman shone his flashlight in the car window. She rolled down the window. He said, "Don't be afraid, Miss. I'll take you home."

Connie began to cry. "But what happened to my boyfriend?"

The policeman said gently, "Don't worry about that right now. Just come along with me, but don't look back."

Connie turned around when she got out of the car and screamed. Her boyfriend was hanging from a tree, a hook in his neck. His bare feet dangled over the car, toenails scratching the roof as he swayed in the wind.

Not only teenagers encounter Mr. Hook. One dark night a family had car trouble on Interstate 10, so they pulled off onto a side road at the next exit. The father parked under a tree and left his family to go for help. He warned his wife and children, "Do not open the car doors or get out for any reason."

No sooner had the father left than a persistent scratching noise came from the car roof. The mother cuddled the children close to her and said, "Don't worry, darlings. It's just the wind. Daddy will be back soon."

In the early morning hours a patrolman called through the window, "Your husband sent us to get you. Don't look back!"

The relieved woman bundled up her children and got into the patrol car. Then she glanced back, only to see her barefoot husband hanging from a tree, his toenails scratching the car roof. She glanced over at the patrolman and exclaimed, "You aren't a policeman!" He smiled diabolically as she stared in horror at the hook on his arm.

Highway 666 isn't the only Arizona road with a specter. Almost every state has several versions of the story of the vanishing hitchhiker (one of the most widely reported legends in modern American folklore) and Arizona is no exception. Vanishing hitchhikers prowl roads in our state and nearby Mexico in many forms.

Around the turn of the century, a wealthy Nogales man known as Señor Robles found himself to be quite a favorite with the ladies. Forgetting the aphrodisiac power of money (made through legal and not-so-legal endeavors), Robles began to believe in his own charm. He neglected his hard-working wife, their seven children, and the dangerous rumblings of angry, cuckolded husbands.

One night while driving down Nogales's San Marcos Street, Señor Robles saw a beautiful woman approaching. Robles thought, well, this is a chance for a little affair of the heart. He stopped the car and the lady got in, ever-so-carefully lifting her skirts just above the ankles.

The woman asked for a match, but Robles, being ever the *caballero*, offered to light her cigarette for her. As he leaned toward her with the lit match cupped in his hand, he got the shock of his debauched life: The woman had no face. Only then did Robles notice the horrible stench of sulphur that permeated the car. Not daring to ask Death to leave, Robles jumped out of the vehicle and fainted. After two weeks of loving ministrations by his wife, he recovered. Never again did his wife or children lack for attention.

Two spectral nuns are known to walk along the Tucson–Nogales road late at night. Once, a rancher pulled over to pick them up, and they got in the back seat. When they informed him of their destination, he couldn't quite make out what they said, so he stopped to let them out at a nearby convent. He turned to the back seat to tell the nuns goodbye, but they had vanished.

A friend—unfortunately, I cannot remember his name—once told me a story about driving near Holbrook on a cold, rainy night. He said he saw a pathetic figure huddled by the side of the road, and pulled over to pick the hitchhiker up. The figure got in the car but said nothing for several miles. At last the ghost said, "Jesus is coming again." My friend asked, "What?" and turned to see an empty seat.

One August day several years ago, a young woman and her mother were driving along Interstate 10 between Phoenix and Casa Grande when they saw a stranger with long white hair and a beard who was wandering along the road. He was not hitchhiking, but they felt compassion for anyone walking in the desert on a hot summer day, so the young woman pulled over and offered to give him a ride. He thanked them and got in the back seat. After awhile he asked if they knew the Spirit of God. Both said yes. Then he asked if they were right with God. The mother turned and said that she did not care to discuss religious matters. The man said nothing more. The mother turned again to ask where he was going and where he wanted to get out. Her daughter had been driving about seventy miles an hour since they picked him up and had not stopped, but the rider was gone.

Mormons have their own version of the vanishing hitchhiker. In a story specific to Arizona, a young Mormon farmer from Safford had a supernatural experience while he was doing genealogical research. In the Mormon faith, it is essential that one's ancestors, through at least four previous generations, are baptized as Mormons, but the man's obligation was unmet as his research had come to a dead end. Driving home from church, where he had been checking some records, he picked up an old man carrying a newspaper. The young farmer mentioned his genealogy problem. The hitchhiker commiserated with him and then asked to be let out at the edge of town. When the young man stopped, he was surprised to see that his rider was already gone. Only the newspaper remained on the seat. Even more surprisingly, the newspaper was an old issue from England. When the young man turned to the obituaries, he found one of his missing ancestors.

Finally, it's no surprise to find that Route 666 has a vanishing hitch-hiker of its own. Many years ago a man was driving along 666 between Morenci and Safford with his pregnant wife. They were on their way to the Morenci hospital for the birth of their first child, and, as you might expect, the man was terribly excited. Driving far too fast, he lost control of the car on one of the switchbacks and plunged the car into a deep canyon. He and his wife died instantly.

To this day, if you drive this stretch of road, you may chance upon the man's ghost, which climbs up to the road every night and hitchhikes a ride into town to find his lost wife. If you give him a ride, you won't hear his voice, for he won't speak a word. You won't see his face, either, for it's concealed by a tall, old-fashioned collar and a pulled-down hat; some say he doesn't have a face at all, only a skull. When you reach Morenci, he will simply disappear. The man is doomed to travel for eternity.

chapter 5

Evil Spirits

A few years ago on the Day of the Dead, a time when the spirits of the dead roam the earth, a vague but sinister face appeared in the shadowy plaster above a doorway in Prescott's Yavapai County Courthouse. All who noticed it tried to make out who it looked like, and many local lawyers insisted that it resembled clients from their past. Was the face really a ghost? Upon further investigation, it was discovered that a plasterer had patched a hole over a vault in a third floor office. He had filled it with wadded paper and then covered the paper with new plaster. As the plaster dried, it lost its smoothness, taking on characteristics that evoked a frightful haunting portrait.

You might conclude that the whole situation was born of overreaction, but given the history of Arizona courthouses, ghostly suspicions were more than appropriate. Like many old Arizona courthouses, the one in Prescott, around the turn of the century, also housed the jail, and even now employees working late hear the rattling of handcuffs and the clanging of shackles. Sometimes at night they see the ghost of a judge who died of a heart attack in his office in the 1950s, walking the halls in full billowing

43

robes. Maybe that face above the door was more than just shadows in plaster, after all.

Ghosts of violent criminals haunt Arizona courthouses seeking to wreak mayhem on those who pronounced the terrible words, "You are hereby sentenced to hang by the neck until dead, and may God have mercy on your soul." Though the unearthly rattling of handcuffs makes for interesting anecdotes, there are three Arizona criminals in particular who capture the imagination as ghosts. Dennis Dilda's evil spirit still struggles to kill anyone who gets in his way—even those who do him a good turn. Bill Brazelton still guards his cache of gold, with a horrible mandate for those who would steal it. George Smiley's ghost seems to have seen the evil of his ways; now he commits only minor mischief.

In the autumn of 1885, W. H. Williscraft hired Dennis Dilda to work his ranch along Walnut Creek about forty miles out of Prescott. When Dilda complained that he could not run the ranch alone, Williscraft hired James Jenkins to help him. The young Jenkins arrived packing a large sum of money, including funds for home passage to England. Unfortunately, he showed Dilda the money.

When Williscraft returned to the ranch in December, he found that someone had broken into his personal trunk, and his pocket watch was missing. When he inquired as to Jenkins's whereabouts, Dilda explained that Jenkins had taken ill and gone to the Prescott hospital.

Williscraft rode into Prescott, making inquiries along the way, and learned that Dilda had been seen sporting a new pocket watch. At the Prescott courthouse, Williscraft swore out a warrant charging Dilda with petty larceny. While in town, he learned that Jenkins had never been in the hospital.

Williscraft and Deputy Sheriff John H. Murphy rode out to the ranch to serve the warrant. Along the way, several men warned them that Dilda was armed and dangerous. At the ranch they found only Mrs. Dilda with her two children. She told Murphy that Dilda had gone hunting. Williscraft and Murphy left, but later that evening Murphy returned alone to serve the warrant. When Murphy did not return, Yavapai County Sheriff William Mulvenon formed a search posse.

On December 22, the posse found Murphy's body in the cellar at Williscraft's ranch home. Digging through rock and dirt, they also found Jenkins's body. Mrs. Dilda broke down in tears and said that her husband had forced her to help him bury the bodies, but that she was not responsible for the murders.

Sheriff Mulvenon organized a second posse and rode out on an extensive manhunt. Mulvenon learned that Dilda was wanted dead or alive for murders in Texas and New Mexico. His brother-in-law had disappeared. The family felt certain that Dilda killed him, but they could not prove it.

The posse tracked Dilda to Henry Walter's place near Ash Fork, where they found him sleeping off a drunk in a ditch. Murphy's hat covered Dilda's face, and he had the deputy's handcuffs in his pocket.

A lynch mob met the posse, but Sheriff Mulvenon promised them a proper public hanging if they let justice take its course. A jury found Dilda guilty of first degree murder, and on December 31 Judge Shield sentenced Dilda, age thirty-seven, "to be hanged by the neck until dead may God have mercy on your soul."

On the morning of February 5, 1886, the day of the hanging, Dilda took a bath and had a haircut. At county expense Sheriff Mulvenon gave him a new suit of clothes. Dilda ordered a breakfast of chicken, lamb chops, steak, and oysters with peas, potatoes, bread, jelly, coffee, and cake. At 11:00 A.M. he ate another huge meal, which probably consumed the Yavapai County budget.

Dilda rode to the Prescott hanging site sitting on his coffin on a wagon. He was hanged at what is now Willow and West Gurley Streets. Just before he dropped into eternity, Dilda requested a drink of whisky, and Sheriff Mulvenon indulged him.

Johnny Koontz and Billy Giles were charged with taking the coffin on their buckboard to Williamson Valley for burial. Along the way they liberally guzzled tarantula juice to keep their spirits up. When they got into the valley they discovered they had lost the coffin and had to go back several miles to find it.

They may have picked up his body, but they left Dilda's spirit behind. Since then, at night around campfires along Walnut Creek near the site of Williscraft's long-gone house, cowboys hear the roar of profanity and the crashing noises of a terrible fight. Evidently Johnny Murphy is still out to get his man, and Dennis Dilda is still committing mayhem.

The ghost of George Smiley inhabits the old Navaho County Courthouse building in Holbrook, Arizona, which now houses the Navajo County Historical Society. Smiley, who was executed in the courthouse yard, opens and closes doors, steals Christmas decorations, and tips over racks of tourist literature. He is a relatively harmless ghost, especially considering that he hanged as a murderer.

In 1899 Smiley, a railroad worker, shot his supervisor in the back during a wage dispute. The victim, Thomas McSweeney, was survived by a blind widow and three small children. A jury tried, convicted, and sentenced Smiley to hang.

Under the Arizona Revised Statutes, Penal Code, Title X, 1849, Arizona sheriffs were obligated to issue invitations to executions. No guidelines existed as to the form, but Navajo County Sheriff Frank J. Wattron was up to the task.

Wattron had grown up in Missouri, where his parents died when he was just thirteen. His uncle, a priest, urged young Wattron to study for the priesthood, so the boy ran away. After wandering around New Mexico and Colorado, he showed up in 1879 in Holbrook, Arizona, eighteen years old, with five dollars and a deck of cards. He became Navajo County Sheriff in 1896. The tall, handsome sheriff sported a huge black moustache, was always chomping on a long cigar, and exhibited a special talent for profanity.

Wattron approached the task of writing the invitation with a macabre sense of humor. His invitation to the Smiley hanging read:

> Mr. _____ You are hereby cordially invited to attend the hanging of one: GEORGE SMILEY MURDERER. His soul will be swung into eternity on December 8, 1899, at 2 o'clock P.M. sharp.

The latest improved methods in the art of scientific strangulation will be employed and everything possible will be done
to make the surroundings cheerful and the execution a success.
—F. J. Wattron Sheriff of Navajo County

Back in those days, most printing was handled by newspaper presses,
so Sheriff Wattron sent the invitation to the editor at the Holbrook *Argus*.
The *Argus* didn't have the proper equipment to do the job, so the invitation was sent on to the *Albuquerque Citizen*. A reporter saw the text and
wired the contents to the Associated Press. Copies of the invitation went
to newspapers all over the United States and Europe.

An embarrassed President William McKinley complained about the
incident to Arizona Governor Nathan O. Murphy. Murphy reprimanded
Wattron and stayed Smiley's execution for thirty days.

Wattron took care not to let the second invitation get out too early.
It read:

With feelings of profound sorrow and regret, I hereby invite you
to attend and witness the private, decent and humane execution of a human being: name George Smiley; crime, murder.
The said George Smiley will be executed on January 8, 1900 at
3 o'clock P.M.

You are expected to deport yourself in a respectful manner, and any flippant or unseemly language will not be allowed.
Conduct on anyone's part, bordering on ribaldry and tending to
mar the solemnity of the occasion will not be tolerated.
—F. J. Wattron Sheriff of Navajo County

Wattron suggested that the governor form a committee during the
next legislative session to draw up a form invitation for executions.

At the gallows, Smiley said, "I have nothing more to say except
to thank the sheriff and deputies for their courtesies, and I die a Christian." The local priest, Father Dille, prayed as Smiley's body dropped in
the gallows.

Decades later, after the courthouse became home to the Navajo
County Historical Society and the new occupants had experienced the

building's mysterious mischief, a member of the historical society and a clairvoyant decided to investigate. On Halloween night they took a Ouija board into the old courthouse and asked if there was a ghost in the building. The word "George" appeared on the board. Just as the "S" began to form, pandemonium broke out and the interrogators fled.

William Whitney Brazelton's ghost haunts Cat Mountain. Brazelton was a highwayman, and he operated alone. Some would like to credit him with being a Robin Hood, but there is no evidence that he ever gave anybody anything but trouble. He kept his loot for himself. He wasn't from Texas—he was born in Missouri—but he was known as *El Tejano* (the Texan), for in the late 1800s, law-abiding Arizonans thought of bold, bad bandits and Texans as belonging to the same category. And if ever there was a man who was bold and bad, it was Brazelton.

In his address to the Ninth Legislature of the Arizona Territory in 1877, Governor Anson P. K. Safford thundered, "Robbers and highwaymen are a scourge to humanity and should be swept from the earth as remorselessly as the most ferocious wild beast." On this issue, at least, most Arizonans readily agreed with their governor.

In those days, Arizona was full of transplanted Texans who appeared in the territory casting long shadows and keeping a constant lookout for the law. Many made fresh starts, mended their wayward ways, and contributed to the state's rich history. A hefty percentage continued their outlaw habits in this wild, raw land. Brazelton fell into the latter category.

He was singularly handsome, six feet tall with shoulder-length wavy black hair, and exceptionally strong; at one point he had worked as the strongman in a California vaudeville act. He had a macabre sense of humor, which was reflected in the mask he wore during holdups—a white bag with eye holes and a gaping red mouth. Victims always remembered the mask. One writer described it as being one of the most grotesque disguises conceivable.

Around 1875, Brazelton had become well known to New Mexico lawmen for his string of robberies—too well known, apparently. He moved to Tucson, Arizona, got a job in the livery stable of Bob Leatherwood (who was both mayor and deputy sheriff), and bullied another employee, David Nemitz, into giving him a place to sleep and supplying him with food and ammunition. Nemitz also furnished Brazelton with information about stagecoach routes and gold shipment arrival dates.

Brazelton held up the Tucson–Florence stage about twenty miles north of Tucson in early August 1878. The driver, Art Hill, and passenger John Clum, editor of the *Tucson Daily Citizen*, were armed, but they decided they were no match for Brazelton's Spencer carbine and pistol.

About a week later, on August 8, a masked man held up the same stage in the same spot. The driver, Art Hill, yelled, "There he is again!"

The masked man roared, "Yes, here I am again. Now throw down the strong box and throw up your hands!"

This time the passenger list included Pima County Undersheriff John Miller, but like Hill and Clum the week before, Miller took a look at Brazelton's firepower and decided that discretion was the better part of valor. The masked man rode off after helping himself to the gold.

Editor Clum took Pima County Sheriff Charles Shibell to task for losing the robber's trail. However, posse member Juan Elias noted that the robber's horse had a crooked hoof, which he tracked to Dave Nemitz's place. Sheriff Shibell subsequently arrested Nemitz, who confessed what he knew about Billy Brazelton.

The sheriff gave Nemitz the choice of either helping him or being charged with federal mail robbery. Nemitz chose to help the law, but insisted that the posse should not take Brazelton prisoner. They had to kill him so that he could not take revenge.

Nemitz set up a supply rendezvous with Brazelton near Point of Mountain. On the evening of August 19, 1878, Sheriff Shibell and deputies Bob Leatherwood, Charles O. Brown, Charles T. Etchells, and Isaac E. Brokaw took up concealed positions near the meeting place. Within an hour, the posse saw a shadowy figure approach. Sheriff Shibell gave the prearranged signal, a cough.

With no further warning, shots cracked the air, and Billy Brazelton roared, "You sons of bitches! I die, but I die a man!" Then he crumpled to the ground and the night returned to a grim, dark silence.

The posse took Brazelton's body back to Tucson, where they propped it against a wall on Main Street near the courthouse for a couple of days. Children were told to consider it a warning to anyone thinking about making a career of robbery. When Billy's corpse began to stink, the county buried him in Potter's Field.

Though Brazelton's body went to a grave, his ghost still haunts the Tucson Mountains, riding a wide range from the La Canoa ranch, about thirty miles south of Tucson, to Picacho Peak, about forty miles north of the city. Brazelton hid his treasure in many caves around Tucson, but his ghost is most often found standing guard over the fortune stashed in a cave on Cat Mountain. If you are brave enough to hang around Cat Mountain at night, you may hear hoofbeats riding through the mesquite thickets, a horse chomping at the bit, and the jingle of El Tejano's spurs as a shadowy figure on horseback makes its way down to the watering hole.

The cantina near the watering hole used to be a favorite hangout for horse thieves, gamblers, bandits, and cattle rustlers. These fearless banditos shuddered and ordered another drink when the ghost of El Tejano rode past the door. The smart ones at the cantina dared not even look outside, but one evening, a young man called Antonio told his father, "I know where there is a cave in the mountains full of hidden treasure. Tonight I am going to get it. I am weary of being poor all the time."

His father knew there was no use in trying to discourage determined young men full of bravado, and so he did not try to stop his son. Instead, he told his son to show the ghost of El Tejano no fear. "Be sure and look at him when he talks to you," he said.

That night Antonio saddled his horse, picked up two gunnysacks, and rode out. He found the cave, its floor strewn with gold pieces. Quickly he filled one sack. Then a strange chill came over the cave and the words, *"Todo o nada"* (all or nothing), struck terror in Antonio's heart. He looked up at a masked horseman. The figure removed the mask, and Antonio saw that he was headless.

Antonio's worried father found him unconscious on the floor of the cave. He threw his son over the back of a horse and took him home. When young Antonio woke up, he asked, "Where is our gold?"

His father replied, "Son, there is no gold."

Antonio began to rant wildly. Three days later he died.

El Tejano also appears from time to time on an old ranch near Sabino Canyon. The last name of the ranch's owner, José, has been forgotten, but his story has not.

One night José's ranch house door kept opening and closing by itself. The family's German shepherd barked as though someone was outside. José walked around the hacienda looking for what caused scratching noises at the window, but he could not find anyone.

The next morning José's cowboys saddled up their horses and told him that they were leaving. They refused to give him any reason other than they had an encounter with the devil. José's wife and mother decided to move into town.

That night José heard two soft knocks. Disgusted, he gulped down his coffee and went to see who was at the door. A masked man on a beautiful white horse stood nearby for a few moments and then rode off. José thought that perhaps he might have found someone to help on the ranch. He asked the ghost, "Who are you? What do you want?" No answer.

José had had a few shots of tequila, which made him more brave than wise, and so he blustered, "I am not afraid of you!"

The ghost whispered, "Come with me and I will show you my gold. You may have all the gold you want."

The rider pulled off his mask, and José saw that he had no face. José called out to him but received no answer. José felt a deathly cold chill pass over him. He jumped on his horse and fled the ranch.

His wife and mother put the trembling José to bed. During the night, the ghost entered the room and asked, "Why were you afraid of me? You said you were not afraid." In the morning, José was dead.

Billy Brazelton's treasure is still out there, and it's not all that hard to find. Only when it has been claimed will his ghost find peace. If you go looking for it, know that terrible conditions exist for you when you find it. You must face El Tejano. When you begin picking up the gold, he will cackle his ghastly laugh and roar, *"Todo o nada."* As quickly as you pick up one piece of gold, another will appear—and another, and then another. So if you should find the gold on Cat Mountain, you might become very rich—or then again . . . ?

chapter 6

The Wishing Shrine

Downtown areas nationwide have died as city populations spread outward and shopping and business centers moved to urban strip malls. Downtown Tucson is no exception. Some people say that one day the devil came to Tucson, and so the city's downtown isn't dead at all: It is very much alive with ghosts.

There is the story of Pancho, who lived on Seventeenth Street in downtown Tucson where the houses were painted yellow, blue, lavender, pink, or occasionally white, each with a well-tended yard, fruit trees, and its own well. The pungent scent from the pink blossoms of the pepper trees kept insects away, chinaberry trees provided shade, vines of every sort climbed the fences, and all sorts of blooms—roses, zinnias, snapdragons, marigolds—made the neighborhood even more colorful. Although lovely during the day, at night Pancho's street was dusty and dark. The trees made black, twisting, sinister shapes in the moonlight—and then there were other shapes that had nothing to do with the trees.

Pancho and his wife, Martina, had a fine, healthy baby boy. Martina kept their house spotless and fixed delicious meals, including wonderful *menudo* (goat tripe), which Pancho sold for the family income. Pancho should have been happy, but he felt increasingly dissatisfied with his lot in life. He took to partying with a bunch of no-accounts at a no-name, no-good Tucson cantina.

One night as Pancho staggered home, every shrub and tree appeared to threaten him. The words of his dear departed mother came into his head: "Pancho, my boy, do not drink and walk the streets at night. The devil will come and get you."

Pancho's stomach churned with terror as he continued along the street. He glanced over his shoulder and saw a large dog following him. He knew every dog on the street, but he didn't know this one. He walked faster and faster, and the dog kept pace with him. He looked at the dog one more time and saw its huge fangs. The beast grew larger and larger. It bared its fangs and growled a hideous, menacing growl.

Pancho made it to the house and slammed the door shut just in time. He collapsed trembling on the couch, and when he came to his senses, Martina was wiping his fevered brow. In his mind he heard a voice that sounded like his mother's saying, "I told you so."

Pancho knew he had met the devil and had no desire to ever do so again. Martina did not ask, and Pancho never said what he saw that night. He became a loving, dutiful father and husband.

There is also the story of Maria, a girl who lived just a few blocks from Pancho. One night she asked her parents if she could attend a dance at the Carrillo Gardens. They refused her request. In those days parents did not feel they had to explain their decisions to their children, and so Maria's parents did not say why they wouldn't let her go—it is possible they had a premonition of terrible events.

Despite her parents' instructions, Maria and her sweetheart sneaked off to the gardens. While there, an elegant young stranger asked Maria to dance, and she accepted. He was very handsome, and while the other young men clumsily stomped all over Maria's satin slippers, her new partner seemed quite light on his feet.

Maria glanced down and realized with horror that they were floating. Her partner's feet were cloven hooves. She screamed, and a chaperon standing nearby quickly made the sign of the cross. The creature instantly disappeared, leaving behind the foul stench of sulfur.

Then there is the story of *El Tiradito*, the castaway, the sinner, and the downtown Tucson altar to his memory that is known as the Wishing Shrine.

There is a special poignancy about the curious, the mystified, the sick, the demented, and the unmarried who kneel in supplication before the altar of El Tiradito. As one of the few shrines in the United States dedicated to a murderer, the Wishing Shrine possesses a quasi-religious significance. It is not recognized by the Catholic Church, but then, Rome would never be comfortable with such a commemoration. The shrine's swirl of legends and miracles all deal with violence and murder.

The ash-blackened brick enclosure is set back from the street on a dusty lot on the old El Camino Royal, now known simply as Main Street. It is within a few blocks of Seventeenth Street, where Pancho ran from the devil dog, and the Carrillo Gardens, where Maria danced with the devil. The enclosure is usually filled with paper flowers, homemade votives crafted out of jelly jars and tin cans, ancient wax-covered candelabras, and a few faithful folks praying for miracles. Ghosts rise among all those tendrils of smoke on slender rays of light, especially at night, when the barren, ugly, easy-to-miss spot is transformed into a holy place of haunting beauty.

The tradition of the Wishing Shrine is simple. Come to the shrine in the evening and make a prayer while you light your candle. If it burns until morning, your prayers will be answered. Supplicants pray for good children, sinning daughters, restored health, wayward spouses, any kind of spouses, and even luxuriant heads of hair. There should be no expectation of an answer to a prayer for worldly goods. Many miracles have been attributed to the shrine: sight has been restored to the blind, cripples have walked, and wayward daughters have come home and begged forgiveness.

In 1927 the Tucson City Council adopted an official version of the shrine's origin, as related by one of the city's oldest pioneers, Clara Fish Roberts. Roberts told of a young sheepherder, Juan Oliveras, who worked on the Goodwin ranch in the late 1870s. Juan became infatuated with his mother-in-law, who lived in Tucson on Meyer Street. One day Juan's father-in-law surprised the amorous pair during one of their trysts. Seizing an axe, the older man killed Juan and fled to Sonora, Mexico. According to a Mexican custom, people who come to violent ends are buried without ceremony on the place where they fall, and such was the case with Juan, who became known as El Tiradito. The original Wishing Shrine was built over his grave.

There are many other versions of the story of El Tiradito. One starts with a wedding in Magdalena, Mexico. A man by the name of Juan married a widow with a three-year-old boy. Shortly after their wedding, Juan turned to alcohol, and love turned sour. The child witnessed frequent quarrels and the abuse of his mother.

One night Juan came home in a drunken rage. The child hid under the covers, but he could not drown out his mother's screams. A door slammed and then there was silence. The boy found his mother in a pool of blood, dying of stab wounds.

For a few years kindly neighbors cared for the boy, but one day he disappeared from the village. His heart was filled with hatred for his mother's murderer. He wanted vengeance. A trail of clues led him to Arizona, and then to a Tucson cantina on Meyer Street. He struck up a conversation with a man known as Juan.

The boy, now a young man, grinned evilly and pulled out a wicked-looking stiletto. When Juan realized that his companion was the son of the woman he had murdered, he tried to flee, but the avenger stabbed him fourteen times, once for each year he had been deprived of a mother. Then he disappeared into the darkness.

In an 1880 version of the story, a lovely young woman could not decide between her two lovers, the quiet, modest Juan and the dashing, handsome José. Both demanded the señorita's hand in marriage, but she simply could not choose between them. On starlit nights, Juan stood beneath her window and sang sweet, beautiful songs of love. During the day, José captivated her heart with his wild horsemanship and brilliant smile. It was inevitable that the two men would fight.

One night in a cantina, the two men exchanged light taunts, but soon rage welled up in their hearts. They took their quarrel outside, where

José drew a jewel-encrusted dagger and stabbed Juan to death. José fled into Mexico. Juan was buried where he fell, and every night the young woman visited the site, lighting candles and praying that God would take her soul. Some say that her wails still echo through the shrine that was built on Juan's grave.

In another story, an evil ruffian known as Cambrusiano robbed missionaries and mines in Arizona and Mexico. Often he would also kidnap a woman, and when he tired of her, he would discard her, kidnapping another on the next raid. One night he made the mistake of stealing a daughter of a Fort Lowell officer.

Soldiers searched everywhere, but they could not find her. At last in the Church of San José del Tucson they heard a sad moan coming from the loft. It was the young woman, terrified and almost dead. She confessed that Cambrusiano had performed devilish rites on her. When she had refused to go with him, he had threatened to kill her. She ran and hid in the church. The day after she was found, she died, and was buried next to the old church of San Augustine.

Her brother set out to avenge her death. He learned that Cambrusiano would likely be in the cantina on Meyer Street that evening. He waited in the shadows until Cambrusiano appeared. Then he drew his dagger and stabbed the ruffian, enjoying the horror in the dying man's eyes. Cambrusiano was buried where he fell—the site of the Wishing Shrine.

Finally, one story claims that the Wishing Shrine was created by the mothers of wayward daughters who were prostitutes. The mothers would light their candles and pray to the Virgin of Guadalupe for the forgiveness of their daughters' sins. The women pray that all erring girls return home and live righteously. On rare occasions, these prayers are answered.

The Wishing Shrine, built in the late 1870s, originally stood on Meyer and Simpson, a block east of its present-day location. It was moved around 1884. It is not known whether the bones of the dead sinner were moved with it. Like it or not, the Tucson City Council became custodians of ghosts on November 7, 1927, when Teofilo Otero officially deeded the Wishing Shrine and the land it sits on to the city of Tucson.

In the 1920s, the shrine was so ugly that the local newspapers suggested that members of the Rotary, Kiwanis, and Lions clubs, along with local engineers, should make a project of beautifying the site. One cold-hearted soul suggested that because the Wishing Shrine was nothing more than greasy candles and an accumulation of unsubstantiated legends about Mexican bandits and Catholic priests, the Pima County Health Department should destroy it. Not long afterwards, a cross was erected in the center of the altar and glowed with a brilliant light. The same disbeliever explained the sight by saying that little boys had placed candles too close to the cross, causing it to catch fire.

In 1940, volunteers repaired the Wishing Shrine to its present state under the auspices of the National Youth Administration. A U-shaped adobe wall topped with brick surrounds a built-out section that serves as an altar. Old-timers recall that relics stood to the left of the altar, including a small headstone topped with a rough-hewn cross, but they have disappeared in modern times.

In 1971, a proposed freeway would have destroyed the shrine, but a vociferous campaign led by University of Arizona Professor Arnulfo Trejo put the Wishing Shrine on the National Register of Historic Places. Now the federal government is also a keeper of Tucson ghosts.

Stand on any downtown Tucson street corner and look into the eyes of the people. The eyes of the homeless reflect despair; other eyes reflect hope, happiness, slyness, lust . . . the full gamut of human emotions. However, in some eyes you may perceive something so frightening and evil that you instinctively turn away. Having seen that, you won't be surprised to learn that voodoo has been practiced here.

In the mid-1930s Tucson suffered from the Great Depression along with the rest of the nation. The unflappable Edith Stratton Kitt, secretary of the Arizona Historical Society, kept the organization alive by serving as its janitor, researcher, and administrator. Through Kitt, an amazing collection of Arizona memorabilia—everything from silver serving sets to pioneers' moth-eaten red long-johns—found its way into the Arizona Historical Society's domain. However, even Kitt was a bit baffled when a contractor, John Craviolini, brought in a quart Mason jar that he unearthed at 354 South Meyer Street. It contained a tallow candle that had been roughly carved into the crude bust of a man. Pins stuck out through the neck, the temple, and the heart. Clearly, someone knew what he or she was doing when it came to the black art of voodoo.

Stratton asked folklorist José del Castillo to search out the story behind the Mason jar, which has since disappeared. Castillo's investigation didn't start well. Faces froze and mouths closed when he brought up the subject of black magic. People who believed in the art of voodoo—and there were many—refused to talk to outsiders. In fact, a local quack healer claiming he could cure anything by putting toads in a patient's stomach had escaped prosecution, despite all the evidence against him, because none of the locals would testify against him. They feared reprisal through black magic.

Finally, Ignacio Calvillo told Castillo that he knew an old woman who might know something. Doña Concepción lived about a block from where the jar had been discovered. Castillo found her living in a small apartment on Meyer Street. Just as he was about to knock, he heard a voice say, "Come in. I have been expecting you."

The tiny wrinkled lady told him the story of Amilia, who had lived at 354 South Meyer Street, and Juan Mario, the father of three children, who had lived with his wife and family in another section of town. Amilia was very much in love with Juan Mario, but she knew nothing of his wife and children. When she found out about them, Amilia burned candles at the Wishing Shrine, but the candles never burned until dawn.

Amilia finally gave up hope of getting her lover back and lost her mind with grief. At moments she wanted to kill Juan Mario. In her terrible loneliness, she sought the company of the devil. From the wax of her burned-down candles, she fashioned the shape of a man and dug a hole in her back yard. She knelt before the hole and offered the devil a prayer of hate with words too horrible to mention on these pages. She stuck the figure full of pins. With a final pin she pricked herself and drew blood, and then stabbed her perfidious lover in the heart. Then she buried the waxen image of Juan.

Castillo asked Doña Concepción, "Did he die of black magic?"

The old woman pulled the shawl around her face and made the sign of the cross.

"And Amilia?"

The old woman's hands trembled, but not from the cold. "It was such a very long time ago," she murmured. "You must go now."

Her parting words rang in his ears. "You may find her praying at El Tiradito." Later, at the shrine, Castillo found a woman in a black shroud murmuring a prayer. He dared not disturb her.

Castillo's notes on his investigation end there. We will never know if he continued to watch the shrine for Amilia, or if he perhaps discovered that Doña Concepción herself was Juan Mario's aged lover. Questions about the black magic remain unanswered, because José del Castillo took the secrets of Amilia to his grave.

A distinct sorrow enshrouds the Wishing Shrine as it continues to attract those who light candles, offer prayers, make wishes, and leave gifts (like locks of hair from women who wished for thick tresses). The site also has a distinct aura of eerie power. One night a bandit robbed the coins left in tin cans there. When he went to bed, there was an insistent knocking at the door. No one was there. The frightened sinner returned the coins, and the knocking stopped.

There are many ghosts here. One is that of a rough, dirty young man who one day hobbled to the shrine on crutches, his foot bound in a dusty bandage. The previous night, he had prayed that his foot would heal. Unfortunately, during the night the flame had been extinguished. The next night he prayed not that his foot would heal, but that he might get a chance to kill the man who shot him in the foot. Once again his candle blew out.

If you should see the ghost of a child, it is Pedro. One day Pedro, a starving six-year-old boy, appeared at the shrine with a candle he bought for a few hard-earned pennies. He lit the candle and prayed that his father might be released from jail so that his mother and brothers and sisters might eat again. The next morning his father came home with money he had saved while in prison. Word got around that Pedro could perform miracles. Then one day he was found cruelly murdered near the Wishing Shrine. His little ghost is the saddest one of all.

Visit the Wishing Shrine and watch the wisps of smoke writhe and contort until they form their troubled specters. A woman exults over the death of her faithless lover. Two men fight for the hand of a lovely señorita. If you have the courage to wait out the night at this site that marks the grave of a sinner, you may even see the ghost of a child who was without any sin at all.

chapter 7

For Sojourners in Search

Arizona is well known for its hospitality to tourists, and tourists in search of ghosts are no exception. Phoenix, the capital of Arizona and the seventh largest city in the nation, is a thoroughly modern place where most houses have been built in the last couple of decades. Even so, Phoenix and its surrounding cities have a phenomenal number of haunts. Hotels, saloons, boarding houses, churches, and restaurants all over the state provide plenty of high spirits.

If you're a sojourner in search of ghosts, you might start at the Oddfellows Club at Southern and Priest in Tempe, which is reputedly haunted—coincidentally enough, it also has thirteen rooms. Casey Moore's Oyster House, which sports the ironic slogan "food, fun, and spirits," would also be a good place to start. The historic building once belonged to William Moeur, brother of an Arizona governor and doctor. Both William and his wife Mary died in the building, and they may be the ghosts that haunt the restaurant. They seem to be very nice ghosts, although there was the time they took chairs that were pushed under a table and turned them to face a window; they scared a dishwasher so bad that he left. Then there was the time a waiter threw his pen out the door and a ghost tossed it right back at him.

Hotel spirits are folks who checked into hotels but never checked out. Really, they should get an afterlife, but if you want to go looking for them in your travels, try booking yourself into Room 16 at Prescott's Hotel Vendome. Ghosts Abby and her cat, Noble, have more or less taken up residence there. One story is that Abby once owned the Vendome, but she had to sell for back taxes. The new owners let her live out her days in Room 16, and she never left, even after she died. Another version contends that when Abby took ill, her husband deserted her on the pretext that he was going out to get her medicine. He never came back, and Abby died of starvation.

One Vendome guest claimed that while she was watching the television show *Sightings*, a ghost story came on and her TV reverted to black and white. It reverted back to color after the program was finished. Another lodger claimed the heat kept going off, but there was no point in blaming the utility company.

A couple of years ago four women took a Ouija board to Room 16 and made contact with Abby, or so they said. Abby told them through the Ouija board that she was thirty-three years old when she and her cat died in 1921. Her husband had betrayed her, and she had no children. The Vendome's owners say Abby will always be welcome. They have no plans to change Room 16.

The San Carlos Hotel in Phoenix is said to have been built over a well of sacred water that had been used by ancient Native Americans to worship their gods of wisdom. Phoenix's first public school was built there, and later the San Carlos, which opened on New Year's Day, 1927.

Less than two months later, a young female hotel guest, Leone Jensen, committed suicide by throwing herself off the roof. Her boyfriend, a bellboy at the nearby Westward Ho, had told her that he no longer loved her and that their hot, impassioned affair was over.

Hotel guests hear strange whispers, feel icy cold drafts, and see doors slam shut and then open by themselves. A bellboy, perhaps Jensen's ex-lover, knocks on their doors and then disappears without even waiting for his tip, giving proof that he is, indeed, not of this world. If he is looking for Leone, perhaps to apologize, he should try the Zane Grey Suite, where a woman walks through the walls while a man paces the floor in another room, coughing and clearing his throat. Guests also report hearing the delightful disembodied laughter of three young boys, who always disappear just as they are spotted running down the hallway.

The Cochise Hotel, a delightful 1882 bed and breakfast in the town and county of Cochise, was about to become a lettuce storage crib in the early 1950s when it was rescued by Elizabeth Fulton Husband. The hotel's turn-of-the-century parlor has a windup phonograph, old walnut furniture, a large mirrored wardrobe, a Wells Fargo safe, and Persian carpets. Husband refurbished the hotel bedrooms with modern amenities such as electricity and plumbing while still retaining an authentic period flavor. Her grandparents purchased the green sofa in the parlor from the estate of Jennie Lind. Possibly Lind, the Swedish nightingale, is the ghost that stalks the halls.

This ghost appeared to a level-headed, retired real estate salesman, George Gardiner, around 1975. When Gardiner and his wife checked in, he asked if they would be the only guests that night. They received a smile and one word from the elderly manager: "Perhaps."

That night, Gardiner looked into the hallway when he heard a strange sob that gave him goosebumps and set his hair standing on end. The weeping had a peculiar quavering sound, as if it came from the other side. What Gardiner saw in the hallway was even more terrifying: a woman's head hung suspended in a ball of light. She had long hair and bright red lips. Suddenly she vanished into a mist and the hall went silent. Gardiner's wife slept through the event, but he can't forget it.

One of Arizona's nicest ghosts is George, who lives in Oracle's one-hundred-year-old Acadia Hotel. In addition to serving as a ghost home, it also functions today as headquarters for the Oracle Historical Society Museum.

In the 1930s many doctors recommended the Oracle climate for consumption (tuberculosis) patients and World War I veterans who suffered from mustard gas poisoning. Subsequently, the Acadia, originally part of a dude ranch, became a sanatorium, complete with a morgue and a post office. Perhaps George is one of those who did not recuperate from the dreadful tuberculosis.

George is always pleasant and never hurts anybody, but back when the Acadia was still an operating hotel, he did give guests and housekeepers a bit of a fright. One night someone tucked a blanket around a guest's shoulders, but when the guest turned on the lights, no one was in the room. This is a typical example of George's friendly behavior.

George isn't the Acadia's only ghost. One evening when the building was still a hotel, an elderly gentleman retired early to the bedroom that had once served as the morgue. He was awakened during the night and swore that a buxom redhead was trying to crawl into bed with him. A female guest also reported seeing a female ghost with flaming red hair wandering the halls dressed in white.

Arizona is home to plenty of haunted houses, among them, Phoenix's Merryweather Mansion. It was built in 1915 by J. Edward Merryweather, who made his fortune in mining, and lived in the house only briefly. The house passed into other hands after Merryweather's death, but remained largely unoccupied. After years of neglect and vandalism, desert growth covered the once elegant pools, gardens, and Grecian columns. Phoenix kids whispered among themselves that the house was haunted. One woman saw a spirit she described as a very handsome man. He was taking an afternoon stroll in front of the house, and she knew that he had no evil intent.

Another Valley haunted house was built around 1922 by a dentist, Dr. Ames, the reputed inventor of dental cement. Ames took great pride in the large, rambling home in the desert south of Phoenix (near what is now Ahwatukee), particularly the home's library and tall bell tower. Dr. Ames was generous to a fault; his servants even had their own private courtyard. Unfortunately, the good doctor died three months after he finished building the house.

The Ames mansion was purchased by a Mrs. Brinton, who lived in the house until her death in 1960. Strange, ghostly noises in the library disturbed her, so she remodeled the house and replaced the fireplace. They apparently went away, and she lived in peace until her death.

During the decade after her death, the house remained empty and at the mercy of vandals. In 1970 several Arizona State University students cleaned up the place and moved in. They claimed to hear Dr. Ames pacing the floor at night. They also heard a little bell ringing in what had been Mrs. Brinton's rooms. Apparently, after Mrs. Brinton had fallen ill, she had been known to ring for the servants with the little bell at her bedside table. When the students would investigate the ringing, the rooms were always empty.

The McCune Mansion, designed by the famous architect Edward Durrell Stone, was finished only a few years ago in Paradise Valley. Philip McCune began construction in 1960 on a dream house to rival the Wrigley Mansion, but he ran into difficulties. McCune's wife divorced him, his financial empire crumbled, and he became ill. In 1971 he was forced to ask for community fund-raising help to complete the house, which was worth about six million dollars twenty years ago. McCune never lived in the house. He spent his last days in the estate guesthouse and died in April 1971. Ghostly visitors, perhaps McCune himself, now stroll along the mansion's terraces and walkways.

The Riordan House in Flagstaff is a thirteen-thousand-square-foot mansion built by the pioneers Timothy and Michael Riordan in 1904. The Irish Riordan brothers had left Chicago to find their fortunes in the rough lumber mill camps of Flagstaff, in the Arizona Territory. They made their wealth in the Arizona Lumber and Timber Company. In 1889, Tim Riordan married Caroline Metz from Cincinnati, and Michael married Caroline's sister, Elizabeth. They were daughters of a prominent Ohio tobacco farmer and merchant.

While in the process of completing the El Tovar Hotel, at the South Rim of the Grand Canyon, Timothy Riordan hired architect Charles Whittsley to design a family mansion, which the Riordan brothers furnished with Tiffany lamps and Gustav Stickley furniture. Massive stone arches flank the porch of this unique forty-room home built of split logs, planks, and shingles. They called it *Kinlichi,* which in Navajo means "red house." Both families lived in the house, but each had generous separate living quarters, joined by a huge billiard room that might be haunted. On special occasions the balls roll around by themselves on the table when no one is playing. No one visible, that is.

Deeply religious, the Riordan brothers incorporated a small chapel in the stair landing where visiting priests said Mass. Caroline insisted that a light in front of the statue of Christ be on at all times. One day while she was away, the light went out. She changed the bulb when she got home, but no light came on. Just as she was about to give up, the light flickered on and then off. That night Caroline died. Those who have seen Caroline's ghost say she still grieves for her daughter, Anna, who died of polio just before she was to be married in 1927.

Blanche, daughter of Michael and the last Riordan to occupy the house, reported that she smelled burning tobacco when no smokers had been in the house, and she often heard the faint clicking of billiard balls. She bequeathed the house and its furnishings to the state of Arizona in 1986.

Even the most dedicated spook spoofers would have to admit that Phoenix's Mystery Castle near South Mountain is unique. In the 1930s, Boyce Luther Gulley learned that he had tuberculosis. He moved to Arizona so as not to burden his wife, Frances, and daughter, Mary Lou. He left them behind in a way that felt like abandonment, but he definitely did not forget them.

When Mary Lou had cried as a child because the tide wiped away her sand castle on the Washington coast, her father had promised her that he would one day build her a real one. Upon his move to Arizona, he began the fifteen-year process of building the castle he'd promised: five stories, eighteen rooms, eight thousand square feet.

Frances heard about the castle for the first time when she received a letter from Boyce in 1945. In the letter he described the location and asked their forgiveness for his desertion. He had recovered from tuberculosis, but he died of cancer just days before his family arrived to visit him. Frances and eighteen-year-old Mary Lou moved to Arizona and took up residence in Boyce's confection of eccentricity.

Over the entrance of the Mystery Castle a sign reads, "The reality of dying was thrust upon him in his prime." A wagon serves as the castle's bar, with room for a "bunk for the drunk." A room called Purgatory separates the bar from the chapel, where modern couples often take their vows between two stone snakes in the floor. Gulley's bedroom contained a love seat from the House of Joy, a brothel in Jerome. In the kitchen, the sink is low to allow a person to sit while washing the dishes.

The stone structure is such a potpourri of unusual stuff that it's no wonder spirits have a high time there. Mary Lou believes that one ghost, who belongs to a beautiful blond lady, was a Texas heiress who frequented the castle in the 1950s. You might see her shadow pass by a window, or catch a glimpse of her on the castle grounds.

Intellectually and culturally refined ghostbusters will be interested to know that spirits haunt the University of Arizona in Tucson and the Phoenix Civic Center. Students have tried to exorcise the spirits at the University of Arizona to no avail. In the university's Maricopa Residence Hall, the ghost of a former coed jingles the locks, searching for what, no one knows. Residents are often unnerved by her eerie gasps during the night.

In the Modern Languages Building a young woman with long raven tresses, dressed in a 1920s style white gown, prowls the hallway and peers into the windows. She is known as the Woman in White and bears a remarkable resemblance to "Little Pinkie," a child model for Sir Thomas Lawrence, court painter to King George III. She appears in a portrait that once hung in one of the building's offices. The Woman in White appeared on campus around 1967. Legend has it that many years ago she was murdered and dumped in a well under the building's foundation.

The modern Phoenix Civic Center was proven haunted when a group from the Phoenix Psychic Research Center spent a night in the Little Theater doing research. They heard strange noises, saw odd apparitions, and witnessed objects moving of their own accord. A piano played, even though nobody except the researchers was in the theater. The researchers held a seance and claimed to have contacted a couple of spirits.

Prescott's old Sacred Heart Church, which now serves as the office of the Prescott Fine Arts Association, has a priestly ghost. Father Edmond Clossen was buried beneath the church altar after his death on June 18, 1902, and now his mischievous presence often haunts the building at night, turning lights off and on, opening closed doors, and closing open ones.

Notwithstanding these visitations, Father Clossen may no longer be buried in the church. The city of Prescott issued a certificate of disinterment and reinterment on September 17, 1969. It listed the minister of Sacred Heart at that date, Father Francis J. Pyka, as Clossen's next of kin. However, there is no record of reburial, and both Pyka and Clossen disappeared from the annals of Prescott history.

All that's left of the church that used to stand at Bell Road and Fifty-Sixth Street is the foundation, an old cemetery, and two ghosts—a preacher and his jealous wife. It seems that the wife became indignant when she discovered her husband with a beautiful young woman on a pew in church one night. The two lovers were *not* praying. The wife lit a fire that consumed the church and the lovers with it. Later, she went insane.

Phoenix's old Indian Graveyard is another favorite haunt. Oddly shaped wooden crosses and unusual burial wreaths appear from time to time on the graves. Bizarre shadows move out of the twilight and wander among the graves, and as the sky grows darker, strange, distant lights begin to flicker.

Bell Butte, a cave situated between two cemeteries, is Tempe's most famous haunt. Years ago archaeologists removed a cache of ancient Native American artifacts from the small grotto on one side of the butte. Since that episode, people of good repute have heard screams coming from the grotto. The mysterious source of these wails at Bell Butte has not been established, but they must be coming from the shaman whose unhappy spirit searches for his medicine bag.

The city of Sedona is situated in some of Arizona's most spectacular country, about one hundred and twenty miles north of Phoenix. Strange radiant discs of light appear in its eastern skies like something out of the *X-Files*. With straight faces, certain Sedonans will tell you that the pilots of unidentified flying objects choose Sedona for a stopover because spaceship fuel is cheaper there. Early stellar bodies to arrive in Sedona include Hollywood movie actors such as Jeff Chandler, who played Cochise in *Broken Arrow*, one of the many Zane Grey movies filmed here.

Today, those who are supposed to know speculate that interdimensional portals exist in Sedona. Sedona vortices are supposed to be the nodes that provide energy to the rest of the earth. In spite of the psychic ruckus caused by the vortices, at least one ghost populates this New Age town. A headless phantom warrior, who changes into a coyote, has taken up residence in a house once owned by Ann Miller, former movie actress and dancer.

Oatman, surrounded by jagged rock spires in northern Arizona's Mohave County, was once a blossoming gold mining center. When the gold ran out, Oatman became the place for the rich and famous to stay when they traveled between Los Angeles and Las Vegas. The town once had two banks, ten stores, a chamber of commerce, and an elegant hotel. Now, except for a few hardy souls making a living from a tourist trade, it's a ghost town.

Oatie, the not-so-famous ghost of the Oatman Hotel, is the happy-go-lucky spirit of a young miner or, according to another version of the story, a cowboy. One night in 1930, he got rip-roaring drunk, as miners and cowboys were inclined to do. As a result, he got himself booted out of the bar. Two days later his body was discovered in a trash heap behind the hotel. Today Oatie has his own room at the hotel, and he keeps the window open no matter how often the staff closes it or how cold it gets.

Oatie also likes his pink chenille bedspread arranged just so or he changes it to suit himself. Guests in this room have seen the doorknob turn by itself and have heard a deck of cards being shuffled. Oatie also makes certain the guest book is open to his favorite page, which changes from day to day.

Movie actors Clark Gable and Carole Lombard were married in Kingman, Arizona, and they spent their honeymoon in Room 15 of the Oatman Hotel. It's pretty cramped, but they didn't mind. Now eerie shadows of their ghosts move along the halls.

Lombard's death, on January 16, 1942, is shrouded in mystery. At the time she was considered one of the nation's most glamorous and gifted actresses. After a performance in Las Vegas, she returned to Los Angeles on a DC-3 plane owned by billionaire Howard Hughes, along with her mother and fifteen servicemen from the army air corps.

Lombard's mother, who had consulted an astrology chart, insisted that the trip would be dangerous that day, but her headstrong daughter insisted on returning to her husband. Shortly after the plane took off, its left wing clipped a mountain outcropping and it nose-dived into a fiery inferno.

Recovering the bodies proved difficult because only horse trails wound up the snow-covered mountain. One of the pack horses, carrying three bodies including Lombard's mother, fell to its death in a deep ravine. Rumors circulated that the plane had been acting strangely during the take-off and that the air force was covering up the crash and concealing sabotage.

Every year over four million tourists visit the Grand Canyon. Everyone feels something primeval when gazing down into its depths. Perhaps some of that is because there are parts of the Grand Canyon that are inhabited by ancient spirits.

Hopis believe that they and all other peoples originated through an opening to the underworld in the Grand Canyon. This is where the ancestral spirits called *kachinas* live after they leave the villages at summer solstice. At winter solstice they arrive again at the pueblos, and the Hopi people hold ceremonies in which masked dancers represent the ancestral spirits who have returned from the underworld.

The mask is the substance of power to the kachina, and this power transforms the individual dancer into a supernatural being—the dancers actually become the kachinas as long as they wear the masks. Kachinas' masks along with their power possess the potential for danger, for occasionally a mask may stick to the wearer's face and kill him. Thus, a faceless kachina is a fearsome thing. While driving at night near the Grand Canyon, if you should notice a kachina with no eyes, nose, or mouth standing by a small fire beckoning for you to stop, just keep on driving.

The Wandering Woman walks the Canyon's North Kaibab Trail. Devastated with grief, this lovely young woman wears a white robe with pink and blue flowers and a shawl over her head. It is said that the Wandering Woman hanged herself in a lodge on the Canyon's north rim in the early 1920s after learning that her husband and son had fallen to their deaths during a hiking accident.

Within the Grand Canyon a number of spots are named Bright Angel, including the Bright Angel Lodge and Bright Angel Trail. Major John Wesley Powell, an early Grand Canyon explorer, is said to have named the Dirty Devil River in Utah after the Prince of Darkness and the Grand Canyon Creek the opposite: Bright Angel. (Curiously, Bright Angel Canyon is listed as the Devil's Spittoon on a 1962 map.)

Quite a different origin of the name Bright Angel was described by John Hance in 1902. Hance was a native of Tennessee who fought with the Confederate Army and then switched allegiances after he was captured. He arrived at the Grand Canyon around 1883. A tourist guide, trail blazer, and raconteur who was known to tip back a few, Hance never let a fib get in the way of a good story. Here's his version of the Bright Angel story, as told to the *Coconino Sun*:

> Yaaaaas! I'll tell ye how it was. We never did know where she come from nor how she got here. All at once she was here and it appeared like she had come to stay. She was sickly; you could see that but she never complained and was always just as dog-gone cheerful as a sunshiny morning! Gad but she was beautiful. She had fluffy hair that was a streak of sunlight streaming through a window and her skin soft as velvet and just white and

pink. She did not look like a person who was intended to live on earth, leastwise in no such outlandish place as this. And the girl was just as good as she looked. The boys all fell in love with her. She used to go down the trail every day, was always looking at the wonderful sights in the canyon with them blue eyes of hers that was like little patches of the sky. Boys used to watch her standing on the rim until she would get to be nothing more than a tiny speck of bright color moving along the rim. Buckey O'Neill, a Grand Canyon promoter, said she was an angel. He knew she was and he turned out to be right because one day she went down the trail and never came back. There was sort of a haze in the Canyon that afternoon. Around sundown the light struck slantwise and it colored like gold. You could not see far into the canyon but Buckey saw something float up through the mist, white and transparent like, but he knew it was her, the Bright Angel and he called the trail Bright Angel.

At Mile 41 on the Colorado River, you will find a plaque erected by a troop of Utah Boy Scouts. It reads:

Bert Loper
1869–1949
Grand Old Man of the Colorado
"I belong to the wondrous West and the West belongs to me."

The spirit of Bert Loper, known as the Grand Old Man of the Colorado, haunts the Grand Canyon. Loper was born in Hite, Utah, in 1869. In 1939, on his seventieth birthday, Loper and a friend, Tom, made a Colorado River trip to celebrate the event. In 1945, Loper developed a gallbladder problem, and his doctor ordered him to stop the river-rafting trips. Loper paid no mind and rafted the Green and Yampa Rivers.

In 1948, he decided to return to the Colorado River and the Grand Canyon. That winter he had a heart attack, and again his doctor insisted that river rafting would be too dangerous. Loper as usual paid no attention, and he set out in a boat down the Colorado. Loper's boat washed up at Mile 41, but searchers never found his body. Today when things come up missing on river trips, river runners have a tendency to fault the spirit of Bert Loper.

chapter 8

From the Ground Up

Arizona's mining history predates the creation of the nation—Native peoples fashioned tools and jewelry from the area's copper, silver, and gold long before the arrival of the Europeans—and is even responsible for the state's name. In October 1736 a Yaqui miner, Antonio Siraumea, discovered a remarkable silver deposit about twelve miles southwest of today's U.S.-Mexico border. Captain Gabriel Beltran called the mine and its small settlement the Real de Arizonac. Before long, the area became known as Arizona (certainly better than Gadsdonia, after the Gadsen Purchase of 1853, as suggested by one politician when Arizona achieved statehood on February 14, 1912). Ghosts of men murdered in Arizona's mining towns and those who met their deaths in mine cave-ins help Arizona live up to being a respectable state of terror.

Tommyknockers immigrated to Arizona with the Cornish "Cousin Jacks" from the coal mines of Wales. (The terms "Cousin Jack" and "Cousin Jennie" came about because so many Cornish relatives worked in the mines together, and they called each other "cousin.") Many Cornish immigrants have mined in Arizona. At the cemetery in Globe, one of

Arizona's primary mining towns, copper plates etched with names like Pascoe, Opie, and Trevillian are attached to the granite headstones. Cornwall natives figure prominently in Arizona's mining history. They include Albert Tallon, safety inspector for Globe's Old Dominion; the huge John Knight family, all of whom worked Globe's Silver King; George Millett, who owned two hundred shares in the Moonlight Mining Company; and two superintendents at the Old Dominion, Samuel Parnell and Frank Juleff.

Tommyknockers are Cornish spirits of those who perished in mining accidents. No more than two feet high, these gossamer ghosts live in the cracks and crevices of mines. They warn worthy people of impending danger by throwing down pebbles; those judged unworthy don't fare so well. Tommyknockers knock over their ladders, trap them in dead ends with no oxygen, and finally pull them into the bowels of hell. It is said on good authority that beautiful, nude female spirits inhabit the same mine crevices. How these two groups get on is beyond the scope of this book.

Be very careful what promises you make when tommyknockers could be listening. Ike and Joe, who worked in the Globe mines in the early 1900s, learned that lesson. One day when they were hard at work in the mine, a barrage of pebbles hit them, and they knew a cave-in was imminent. Ike shouted, "Tommyknockers! Let's get the hell out of here!" and Joe vowed, "I will go to church every Sunday if my life is spared."

The men got out alive, but Joe decided that mining of the underground sort was not for him. He went to New York and became quite wealthy playing the stock market. Ike continued to work the mines and made a fair living for his family.

Years later Joe returned to investigate one of his Globe mining properties. When he went down into the mine he ran into Ike. The two old friends slapped each other on the back and chatted awhile as they walked along, but soon Ike became serious. He asked, "Did you keep your vow about going to church?"

Joe laughed and said, "For about two weeks."

Ike shook his head. "It's no good! A man not keeping his vows!"

Joe said, "You always were too serious." Just then he stepped on a loose plank. Ike gasped in horror as his old friend dropped to eternity. Tommyknockers won't help you if you don't keep your promises.

Ike went on to become one of the best tunnel drillers around. Years later, when times turned tough, a man came to town and offered Ike a huge sum of money to drill a tunnel two hundred feet into the earth. Ike couldn't believe his good fortune. The well-dressed stranger, a handsome but sinister-looking sort, never gave his name, but he deposited a large sum of money at the bank and left instructions with the banker so Ike could draw on it. Not being the selfish sort, Ike thanked God that he could provide for his family and friends.

Ike felt obliged to tell the banker that he did not think there would be any ore in the area where the man wanted him to drill. The banker smiled and said, "Start tomorrow."

Sure enough, they drilled two hundred feet but didn't hit a deposit. Ike consulted with the banker, who said, "Here's more money. Go down another two hundred feet."

Ike joked, "Okay, but what am I doing? Drilling clear to hell?" The banker smiled.

The work became more arduous because the tunnel had to be shored up with timber. Ike and his men drilled another two hundred feet, but still nothing. By similar stages they reached a depth of one thousand feet.

At that point, Ike wanted to make a survey, but the answer came back, "You are forbidden to make any survey! Go back to where you started and drill down two hundred feet, but veer off a little to the left."

The men drilled for awhile but then an old timer came to Ike and said, "No more drilling for me. Jobs is scarce but there's tommyknockers down there. I hear sounds."

"What kind of sounds?"

"Evil spirits. Tommyknockers is warning us!"

One by one the men turned in their resignations. Ike made no effort to stop them because he believed that the project might take a diabolic turn. Ike knew that evil spirits try to pull men deeper and deeper into hell with money and greed—just another two hundred feet, they said, and then another, and another. Ike had no desire to drop into hell. The drilling stopped, and the banker left town.

Even the Globe Ace Hardware store, built in 1888 by the Old Dominion Mining Company to dispense tools to the miners, has a ghost. Employees think his name is Young, and they're fairly certain he must have committed murder. They say he shot someone in the back but claimed self-defense and was released. He particularly likes to show up on dark and stormy nights—but then, what self-respecting ghost doesn't?

Young generally keeps to himself on the second floor among the used tires and the pails set out to catch rain from the leaky roof. He paces back and forth and whistles the same four notes over and over, moving stuff off the shelves and arranging it neatly on the floor. How he got there is not clear, but ghosts do as they please.

No ghosts have bloodier histories than those who reside in Cochise County near what is left of Brunckow's cabin. On two separate occasions, fourteen years apart, murders took place here. All that remains now is the foundation and the ghosts.

Frederick Brunckow, an engineer, received his education at the University of Westphalia in Germany. He had to leave Germany shortly after the 1848 revolution—just why, he never said, but probably his demonstrations as a student during the revolution did not endear him to the government.

About ten years after leaving Germany, Brunckow came to Arizona. He developed a silver and gold mine in Cochise County not far from Tombstone, and built his cabin on the east side of the San Pedro River on a small hill that gave him a view of the surrounding countryside. Travelers loved to visit him, because he understood the science of mining and willingly shared his knowledge with miners and others who were interested, and he was a good cook and a fascinating storyteller.

One night in 1860, one of Brunckow's employees, William Williams, returned to the cabin after making a trip into Fort Buchanan for provisions. He entered the darkened cabin and lit a match—only to discover two bodies soaked in blood. They were Williams's cousin, James Williams, and an assayer named John C. Moss, and they had been brutally murdered by

Brunckow's workers, as had Brunckow. Brunckow's body had been pierced with a rock drill and dumped down a mineshaft. The murderers had taken everything of value and fled to Mexico.

Fourteen years later, more bloodshed occurred at the Brunckow cabin. Milton B. Duffield, a native of Virginia, arrived in Arizona in 1863 as its first U. S. marshal. Duffield stood six feet three inches and wore a silk plug hat, cutting a conspicuous figure wherever he went. No one ridiculed him for fear of getting to know his powerful fists up close. He had a talent for firearms and a bad temper. Many judged him insane; others considered him a ruffian who was best ignored.

After eighteen months on the job, Duffield hadn't been paid, so he resigned and headed for Washington, D.C., with his complaints. After awhile he returned to Tucson, more disgusted and belligerent than ever.

On June 5, 1874, Duffield and Joseph Oligher rode to the Brunckow Mine, which Duffield claimed that he owned. James T. Holmes, who occupied the Brunckow cabin, also claimed ownership to the mining property. Upon seeing Duffield and Oligher, Holmes grabbed his double-barreled shotgun and threatened to kill either of them if they came any closer. Duffield continued to advance, while Oligher, showing better judgement, withdrew. Holmes shot Duffield in the head, and then turned himself in to the sheriff's office. He was released on the basis of justifiable homicide but was eventually brought to trial and found guilty of voluntary manslaughter. The judge sentenced Holmes to three years in the Yuma prison, but he never spent a day there. He escaped from the Pima County jail after seventeen days and was never heard from again.

Duffield was buried near Brunckow not far from the mine. The Tucson *Citizen* wrote: "It is claimed by some good men that he [Duffield] had redeeming qualities. Such may be the case, we are free to confess that we could never find them."

At night, folks camping near the Brunckow cabin see wispy figures drifting between the mineshaft and the cabin, and hear a beautiful Apache chant and drums, or divine music like an angel chorus trying to quiet the site's violent ghosts. The music is enough of an attraction to consider camping in this area, but if you decide to sleep on the cabin foundation, don't say you weren't warned.

One day in the 1880s, Fort Huachuca soldiers scouting southern Arizona's mountains came across a crusty prospector and asked him what he was looking for. He tersely uttered one word: "Gold!"

The soldiers laughed and said, "All you'll find here is your tombstone."

The prospector, Ed Schieffelin—who, oddly enough, was a frequent visitor to Brunckow's cabin when Brunckow still lived there—discovered not gold but a mother lode of silver. Remembering the soldiers' warning, he named his first claim Tombstone.

With the silver strike, prospectors swarmed into the wicked tent city that Tombstone became. By day they made more strikes, including the Lucky Strike, the Tough Nut, the Grand Central, and the Contention, each richer than the one before. At night they caroused with harlots, gamblers, and a variety of other rascals of dubious reputation.

Tombstone is best known for the famous gunfight at the OK Corral, but many more died violent deaths in this town, and it is now home to a large cluster of ghosts—some say at least a hundred. Stroll along Allen Street and you might hear a piano player banging out old-time popular tunes, though you will never see the performer. Gaze into a gilded mirror and see reflections of phantom madams in sequined evening gowns and brilliant jewels. They smile, wink, and disappear.

There have been numerous sightings of an apparition of a lovely young woman in a white dress at the Aztec House, a Tombstone antique shop. In Nellie Cashman's restaurant, high-spirited poltergeists sweep dishes off the tables and drop them with frightening crashes. Occasionally someone sees a man who resembles Wyatt Earp, dressed in a black hat and frock coat, crossing the street near the Wells Fargo Bank, but he vanishes before he reaches the other side. Even Ed Schieffelin, who has an imposing grave marker on Boot Hill, has been known to wander in spirit form through Schieffelin's Hall, where in the town's heyday legitimate stage plays were presented to the better class of citizens.

Big Nose Kate's Saloon was a very popular haunt back then—and it is now, too. Kate dispensed the worst rotgut whiskey in town, but few customers left her place with cash on their person. Also known as Nosey,

Kate Elder, and Doc Holiday's woman, Mary Katherine Harouny and her ladies of the night helped push Tombstone to the far edge of decency. Ghosts of gamblers past still lounge in the doorways at Kate's, belly up to her bar, and knock over beer bottles, perturbed, no doubt, that their afterlives didn't come equipped with church keys for removing bottle caps. Big Nose Kate herself likes to appear from time to time and whisper sexy secrets into men's ears.

At the famous Bird Cage Variety Theater, where the plaintive lyrics to "I'm Only a Bird in a Gilded Cage" were composed, visitors hear the ghostly sounds of cards shuffling and glasses clinking. Women's laughter drifts down from the balcony, which is divided into boxes, or cribs, where soiled doves once plied their trade.

A few years ago the Bird Cage owners installed a life-size mannequin of Wyatt Earp in one of the balcony boxes, and strange things began to happen. Every night Wyatt would have his hat on, and every morning the hat was found on the floor. Perhaps he simply didn't like his seating arrangement, for when they moved him to an end box where a pretty mannequin of a lady of the night waited, he seemed much more content, and his hat stayed on. Before the fight at the OK Corral, Wyatt and his friends sat at one end of the theater, while the Clantons, the MacLaurys, and Sheriff Johnny Behan sat at the other end. Perhaps the owners had seated Wyatt at the wrong end of the theater. One must be careful with such ghostly protocol.

While not quite as famous as Tombstone, the mining town of Jerome was just as sinful, and it also hosts a cluster of ghosts. Today Jerome is a ghost town located at the top of a series of switchbacks. Its couple dozen buildings cling precariously to a steep slope, and its couple hundred hardy souls make their living off a good tourist business. Jerome's buildings have always moved along the hillsides; the town's famous travelling jail slid three hundred feet. On the night the theater slipped two feet, the audience inside kept watching the movie with rapt attention. The movie was the only excitement in town.

Jerome's United Verde Hospital opened in 1927 and closed in 1950, when the mines closed. Even during its years of operation the hospital had a reputation for being haunted. Coughing, gasping, moaning, and cries of pain emanated then and now from empty rooms. The shadowy figure of a man wandered the halls, turning the nurse call buttons on and off.

The hospital reopened in 1996 as the Jerome Grand Hotel. The preeminent ghost of this establishment is Claude Harvey, who was born in Scotland and worked as the hospital's fireman and engineer from 1931 until his death. Harvey died under mysterious circumstances: His head was pinned under the hospital elevator one fine April morning in 1935. Since that tragedy, fans and elevator lights have come on and gone off on their own, doors have mysteriously locked and unlocked themselves, and footsteps of a ghost have been heard pacing up and down the halls. Also, the building's original elevator has sounded on occasion as though it were going up and down, even though it has been parked on the top floor since 1950. In July of 1997, a guest's bathroom door slowly opened all the way by itself as he watched; he retreated to the lobby, where he slept on a couch until daybreak.

At its peak, Jerome boasted over one hundred ladies of the night, many of whom still haunt the town. For the most part, these women were known only by nicknames like Fat Fanny, Big Bertha, Cuban Mary, Frenchy, and Madame Pearl. Jennie Bauter is one of the few for whom we have a last name, and she is one of Jerome's most celebrated specters.

In her youth Jennie was beautiful, fiscally savvy, and in her own way, quite powerful. Once when a fire broke out at Jennie's place, she solicited the volunteer fire department with an offer that they could not refuse. If they put out her fire, she would give them free lifetime passes to her establishment. Men who worked for the fire department (and men who did not) charged up Jerome's treacherous hills and put out Jennie's fire in no time.

Jennie became one of Jerome's wealthiest madams. She also set up a bordello in Goldfield that fared quite well. Jennie had fourteen thousand dollars in the bank by the early 1900s, but years of heavy drinking, prostitution, and hard living ruined her beauty. She sought solace in the opium dens and took in a scoundrel of a lover by the name of Clement C. Leigh. The forty-three-year-old Leigh had worked in the mining camps along the Colorado River before becoming a San Quentin alumni, thanks to a knifing incident that narrow-minded law enforcement officials insisted on calling murder.

On the morning of September 2, 1905, Leigh was drinking heavily in Jennie's saloon. (In those days, saloons were open around the clock.) He told his fellow sots that he intended to get his hands on a large amount of money, even if he had to kill to do it. He marched up to Jennie's room, kicked in the door, and demanded money. She fled, but Leigh followed her out into the street, where he shot her three times. Before the horrified gathering of onlookers could stop him, Leigh shot her again in the head. He would later claim he did it to put her out of her misery.

Leigh then fired into his own chest, laid down beside Jennie, pulled his hat over his head, and waited to die. But he did not die. Mohave County Deputy Sheriff Fred Brown rescued him from a mean mob intent on a lynching, and took him off to a safe jail in Kingman. On October 15, 1905, Leigh was sentenced to hang for his crime.

The town of Goldfield gave Jennie a big, splashy funeral, after which her spirit returned to Jerome with the ghost of her cat. Today the Inn at Jerome has turned Jennie's brothel into a Victorian hotel with eight rooms, including one called "Spooks, Ghosts and Goblins." Jennie's cat has the run of the place. Should you find an indentation on your pillow, Jennie's cat probably slept there. If you feel cold air around your legs, her cat brushed against you. Jennie visits the kitchen often and drops things just to let you know she's still around. Her residence of preference is the Lariat and Lace Room, where she continually rearranges the furniture and turns the ceiling fan off and on. In the late evening, she walks the streets keeping her eyes on the ghosts of her girls.

Douglas, Arizona, once home to a large copper smelter, has had its fair share of the rough and rowdy. In its early days, the town's elegant Gadsden Hotel, with a lobby replete with marble pillars, hosted visiting mining executives. Although the executives were generally less rowdy than the miners, they did leave spectral footprints. But it is the ghost of a soldier boy who for the past twenty-five years has proved most intriguing. He may be a soldier who fought with General John Pershing when he went in search of Pancho Villa, or he might be a hotel guest who perished when fire destroyed the original Gadsden Hotel in 1928.

The soldier ghost usually visits the hotel around Lent, for some un-known reason. (There's no other evidence that his ghost is particularly re-ligious.) While lounging in the comfortable chairs in the lobby, guests have suddenly had their conversations interrupted by strange whispers as a cold, clammy feeling enveloped them. Guests and employees have also seen a headless soldier wearing a khaki shirt and pants who wanders around the basement and then goes upstairs and walks down the corridor and straight through a locked wrought-iron gate without so much as asking, "Please, may I have the padlock key?" If he gets to a dead-end corridor, he simply goes through the walls. Of course, not everyone admits to seeing a man; some see just shadows.

Not far from Douglas is the historic copper town of Bisbee, which hit its boom when the invention of electricity created a demand for copper wires. Everybody in town knows the Copper Queen Hotel is haunted, but who is the ghost?

This strange lady in a long, black or red dress wanders around the hotel stopping clocks. She appears in the bar, then disappears and reap-pears. If only men are around, she appears naked on the staircase, clutch-ing a glass of whiskey. Hmm . . . wonder what she did for a living? It's hard to convince men how dangerous it is to go with her when she whispers en-ticing promises in their ears.

In Room 309, windows open by themselves and the room may become very cold, even in hot weather, if the ghost has decided to check in for the night. A little boy wrapped in a towel may appear and suddenly disappear, and yet no one admits to any missing kids. The tele-phone rings and a voice asks for Howard, a clerk who worked for the hotel in 1910.

Perhaps the strangest mining spirit to roam the Arizona desert is that of Ollie Englebritson. Ollie was born to a seafaring family in Norway. His sweetheart, Ingrid, wanted him to break the seagoing tradition because both of their families had lost men to the sea. Ollie loved Ingrid, but when his father died, he knew no other way to make his living than the one handed down to him.

One night an Atlantic gale battered Ollie's small freighter, and he heard a voice say, "You will die by drowning." The freighter was tossed about, and several crewmembers were nearly lost, but Ollie helped save them and they all made it to shore.

Not being a superstitious man, Ollie forgot about the warning and continued to go out to sea. On another stormy night, he again heard the voice whisper, "You will die by drowning." Nothing serious happened, but Ollie decided that perhaps he should not push his luck. In America he could make a new life and send for his beloved Ingrid.

Parting for the young couple was hard, but both decided that it would be for the best. Ollie sailed to San Francisco without any mishap. After clearing customs, he saw a sign that someone translated as, "Wanted: Strong men to work the mines in Chloride, Arizona."

Ollie went to Chloride. He didn't mind when the other miners laughed at the way he spoke. He went on the yob and worked a yack-ammer and he yumped, by yiminy, over a dry wash, to work on the cabin he was building for Ingrid on the other side.

Ollie did very well in the mines. The warnings disappeared. The cabin was finished, and he knew Ingrid would love it. He had saved enough money to send for his sweetheart.

Now, Chloride is so hot and dry that frogs live to a ripe old age without learning to swim. Birds use potholders to pull worms out of the ground. Not surprisingly, it had been many years since the dry wash next to Ollie's cabin had seen flowing water.

Coming off his shift one evening, Ollie watched the monsoon clouds build up. He was happy and thought only of the future with his Ingrid. Then he heard a roar down the wash, and a dreadful voice whispered, "You will die by drowning."

A few days later his friends found his body. Ollie Englebritson had drowned in an Arizona flashflood. His spirit continues to wander the dry Chloride gullies, warning others of floods during the monsoon season.

In 1900, Kentucky Camp, near present-day Sonoita, showed promise as a gold mining operation. James Stetson and a man by the name of McAvery, from San Jose, California, organized the Santa Rita Water and Mining Company to work Kentucky Gulch by hydraulic methods. Impounding dams were built in nearby Gardner and South Canyons. Still, they never could get enough water to make Kentucky Camp a viable operation. In 1905, Stetson fell or was pushed out the third story window of Tucson's Santa Rita Hotel and plunged to his death. McAvery died the same year.

Today Kentucky Camp is a favorite spot for hikers. At night a light goes on in the main headquarters. Trouble is, there's no electricity in this building. Perhaps the ghosts of Stetson and McAvery are working late, trying to find a way to appease wrathful stockholders.

The Superstition Mountains have a reputation for possessing a supreme heart of darkness. Misty cold clouds appear in a blue sky and follow hikers. Bizarre gusts of wind drive people off the narrow ledges. Certain caves and crevices cannot be photographed. Apaches claim there is an ancient society of Native American people guarding the gold in the mountains, and avoid certain areas near a peak known as Weaver's Needle that they consider abominably evil. This area is one of the entrances into the hereafter from which there is no return.

Around 1878, Jacob Waltz staked a claim on a rich gold vein in or near the Superstitions. Many people tried to trail the Dutchman to his mine, but none succeeded. Several are reputed to have died by his hands. He left tantalizing clues about the location, like this one: "From the tunnel of my mine I can see the Military Trail below, but from the Military Trail you cannot see the entrance to my mine." To this day, many seekers have become obsessed with finding the Lost Dutchman's treasure in the Superstition Mountains.

James McDonald, a geologist, wrote a story in the *Arizona Daily Star* about a terrifying meeting he and an old prospector by the name of Drussard had with the Dutchman's ghost. It seems that after a run of bad luck with prospecting the Pinal Mountains, Drussard decided to make one last trip into the Superstitions to see if he could find the Dutchman's gold.

McDonald tried to dissuade him. Drussard said, "Didn't I see him blowing in money in Phoenix and don't I remember it as well as if it was yesterday? I can never forget him, for if ever the devil was pictured in a human countenance, that face was the Dutchman's." McDonald decided to go along.

After several days of wandering the Superstitions, McDonald became discouraged when he saw that geological conditions did not portend finding great quantities of gold. Moreover, he found the area's desolation depressing—though it didn't seem to have an effect on Drussard.

The pair came upon several old trails that led nowhere, and Drussard was particularly puzzled. Trails that are made by people lead from one place to another. These trails seemed to be made by gnomes long ago as a practical joke on inquisitive mortals who wished to unravel the secrets of the Superstitions.

Then one day the men followed a trail that took them to a cabin. Drussard supposed it might be the Dutchman's cabin. The one-room structure had a fireplace about which were strewn rusted pots and pans. In the middle of the room was a rough-hewn table with three chairs. The way the room was arranged made it look as if the cabin had been deserted only a short time ago, but a deep layer of undisturbed dust indicated it had not been inhabited for years.

Drussard said, "What gets me is that while the place has not seen a man for twenty-five or thirty years, everything is as solid as when it was built, and the animals have so much respect for it that not even a spider has cast a web on the walls. Rattlers like such places as this to live in but there is not a track of a rattler in the dust, and as there is not a snakeskin around, it shows that no snake has been here. Funny old hills these Superstition Mountains."

McDonald wanted to get out of the place, but Drussard insisted on sleeping in the cabin because a storm was brewing. Thunder boomed and lightning threw a hideous glare through the chinks in the cabin walls. Then rain came down in torrents. Gusts of wind tore through the cracks with an uncontrolled fury. Shrieks and howls not human mingled with roars of thunder.

Finally both men fell into a restless sleep. McDonald awakened with a start. A sickly yellowish light filled the cabin. Sitting at the table was an old man dressed in the mountain man garb of forty years earlier: buckskin shirt, leather leggings, light-colored slouch hat. His body was small and his head grotesquely large. He resembled a German gnome, but his face did not reflect the good humor or generosity associated with gnomes. His nose was long and hooked and his beady eyes were avaricious. His face expressed brutality and intemperance.

A young man stepped quietly forward and emptied gold ore and coins from a sack. McDonald wondered how another person could have entered the cabin without his noticing. Very soon the two men appeared to argue, but no sound came from their lips. McDonald got the impression that the young man wanted the old man to leave the mountain, but he was loathe to do so. The old man caressed the gold as if it were a woman he loved.

Then McDonald saw an Apache woman standing in the doorway. Her nose was cut, signifying that she had violated the moral rules of the tribe. Her hideous features made her the perfect consort for the old man. Whenever the old man agreed with his young visitor, her face took on a fearsome aspect and she pulled a knife from her bosom. When he disagreed, she smiled and withdrew the knife. Finally the old man agreed to leave. Like a flash, the harridan crossed the room and drove a knife into his back. He collapsed on the floor with mouth agape and eyes open.

At that point Drussard screamed. The Apache woman advanced on him. McDonald closed his eyes, fully expecting to be swept into hell. When he opened them, only he and Drussard were in the cabin.

McDonald said, "That was a terrible dream!"

Drussard retorted, "Hell, that was no dream. That was the Dutchman!"

Many years ago, a diary from 1883 was discovered along the banks of the Colorado River in La Paz County, about two or three days north on horseback of where the Gila River joins the Colorado. It passed through many hands and many years before it was made public in California, bringing to light a murder:

Blood is on my hands! A blur of crimson before my eyes! The skies are blazing before me. The sun is sick with gore. The winds from the desert shriek at me—shriek and howl: and this one word only do they wail in my ears—this dreadful word. Murderer!

It all comes back to me now. It is seared in my brain. The long search for the mine; the days in the desert, in the mountains; and then, behind that hill that overlooks the Valley of Death the vein of white shining silver—wealth for a king.

Then it swept over me—my years of poverty and toil. The cold of the rich as they saw my penury—and here was my wealth. I would have it all— all! Not even my partner would share the treasure. He stooped to pick up the precious metal and I struck him, him the friend of my toils and the one who never failed me, him who shared his food with me, who had slept upon the desert and in the mountains under the same blanket; who had nursed me when I lay in sickness—I struck him down God! I was mad. I had not thought of the cold still face that would lie there under the blow.

Should you go hiking in this area and hear mad ravings or run into a miserable-looking soul, know that you have encountered what is surely the most tortured spirit that Arizona's mines ever produced.

chapter 9

Native American Spirits

Arizona is home to twenty-three Native American tribes, and these residents are no exception to the rule that all Arizona cultures have stories of mysterious events.

For as long as anyone can remember, the people of the White Mountain Apache Reservation have known about and believed in the existence of three male ghosts who haunt the eighteen-mile stretch of highway from White River to Pinetop, known locally as "the Hill."

One morning when Lori Davisson was working as a historian at the Fort Apache Culture Center, a staff member came to work telling of a terrifying experience she had late the previous evening as she drove down the Hill. She looked in her rearview mirror and saw three men in the back of her pickup truck. She drove faster and faster, trying to get rid of her three mysterious passengers, frantic to reach home and safety in White River. When she reached the bottom of the Hill, she looked back and discovered that they had disappeared. A year later Davisson, who is now with the Arizona Historical Society, was researching White Mountain Apache History. She learned that around 1850 there was a feud between members of the

White Canes Clan and the neighboring Red Rock Strata Clan. Anna Price, daughter of a White Mountain chief who witnessed the fight, told the story of the feud and the origin of the ghosts to anthropologist Grenville Goodwin.

One day the White Mountain people living around White River saw several men from the Red Rock Strata Clan pass by and then ride up the Hill. The White Canes men painted themselves for war and followed them. Not long afterwards, three men were seen descending the Hill. They disappeared before they reached the bottom. Later, the White Mountain people learned that the White Canes men had overtaken the Red Rock men, and in the ensuing fight three White Canes men were killed. The Apaches believed that the three men seen coming back down the hill were the ghosts of the men killed in the battle. That belief persists to this day.

Coal Mine Canyon is a place of many changes. In ancient times a tremendous combustion caused the coal layer below the rim to burn with such intensity that the shale turned a deep crimson color. Where natural chimneys formed in the rocks, the shale melted and flowed into the rock crevices and now the canyon is filled with long pink, tan, and green spiral formations that contrast dramatically with the red sandstone. Eons ago the canyon was a shallow body of water surrounded by sand and swamps that produced fossilized oyster shells, which Navajos call Red Mother's toenails. Fossilized leaves and twigs suggest that once a giant redwood forest covered this part of Arizona.

Native Americans and Anglos alike have seen an amorphous white shape rise high over the canyon and form the milky figure of a beautiful young woman. Navajo legend claims that once when a young couple and their child walked along the canyon rim, the father and child stumbled and fell to their deaths. The grief-stricken young woman returned to the spot every night until her death, and now she continues to return on full-moon nights.

For many years coal has been mined below the rim of the west fork of the canyon. Whenever the coal miners hear a knocking sound at night, they look into the canyon and see an aura that they believe indicates that somebody had just died. They wait and watch for a few moments until the white woman begins her dance around the canyon. Then they grab their blankets and head for home.

Hopis believe that the milky figure in Coal Canyon is *Quayowuuti*, Eagle Woman, who over one hundred years ago became deranged and wandered from her home in Old Oraibi. She rested along the trail to another Hopi village, Moencopi, on the rim of Coal Canyon. Her son tried to persuade her to return home, but she refused. In her lunacy, she imagined that she saw kindred spirits, and she reached out to them, overstepping the cliff and falling to her death.

Her family and friends buried Eagle Woman in the traditional Hopi manner. With rocks they covered her corpse, which lay where she had fallen, and placed a digging stick near at hand so that she could climb out and proceed to the other world. On the fourth day after her burial, Eagle Woman climbed out of her grave and wandered into Coal Canyon. From that time forth she has come out to dance on the nights of full moons. Hopis fear her, but occasionally brave souls will leave food out for her. On the day Eagle Woman returns to Old Oraibi to dance in the plaza with her people, perfect harmony will be restored to the world.

Navajos bring their sick to Coal Canyon to be cured. They believe that if the misty woman dances to the north, the sick one will be cured, and good things will happen to the tribe. If she dances to the south, death and misfortune are inevitable.

One old Navajo man, suffering from an incurable disease, asked his family to take him to the rim of Coal Canyon, where he wanted to die. The family built a brush shelter for him and left, resigned to the idea that the grandfather's days on earth were over and he should meet death on his terms. The old one patiently waited to join his ancestors, but his health began to improve, and within a few weeks he was walking around. One day a figure appeared and beckoned the old man to follow her. His stunned family watched as the old grandfather returned to the village, healthier than ever, to live another eight years.

In Begashibito Canyon in northern Arizona's Navajo County dwells a Navajo spirit who helps lost travelers of every walk of life. Begashibito Canyon is also home to another helpful spirit, a Franciscan priest.

Many think the latter spirit, who has been seen wearing a Franciscan's robe tied with a rope, is the ghost of Fray Hernando de Escalante, who explored Arizona's Hopi villages around 1774. He may have been among the first Europeans to cross the Colorado River. When he discovered ears of corn near Oraibi, he gave thanks to God and asked that good spirits protect the region and its people from all harm.

One Navajo woman saw Begashibito's Good Spirit clad in a beautiful Navajo blanket with a band around his forehead and bear grass sandals on his feet. He came to her in the midst of a torrential summer storm that was roaring through the canyon. The woman was stranded with her horse on a precarious steep ledge. She could scarcely see through the rain beyond her horse. At first she grew uneasy, and then terror gripped her. But then she heard above the noise of the storm a unique sound—not loud or soft, just different from the sounds of the storm. It almost sounded like a voice. She tried to discern words, but a crackle of light rent the skies and a thunderclap left her trembling. Just as she was about to despair of her life, she saw the man with the blanket. Then she knew. She was hearing the Good Spirit, and he was telling her to follow him.

No sooner had she ridden out of the wash when she heard a mighty roar. She watched as a great wall of water crashed down the arroyo where she had been riding. Nothing would survive this flood. She turned and looked again for the Good Spirit. He turned his kind, weathered face and smiled before disappearing into the mist.

Hosteen Black Goat also owed his life to the Good Spirit. He found himself in the swirl of a sandstorm while riding through Coal Canyon. His frightened horse spooked and reared, but Hosteen held on. Suddenly there appeared a clear path through the sand. He got the impression that someone was walking ahead of him. Finally the figure of a man came into focus. The horse quieted down, and Hosteen gave it the reins. The Good Spirit led them out of the Canyon to safety.

Hosteen Tsosie's three small children wandered away from their mother's sheep camp during the shearing season. By nightfall the children had not been found, and the neighbors joined in the search. At dawn a party of searchers found the three children unafraid and walking toward their mother's camp. They were none the worse for their ordeal. When asked how they found their way home, the oldest boy said, "An old man in a long gray coat told us to follow him, and we did." The adults whispered to each other, "It was surely the Good Spirit of Begashibito."

Anglos have also felt the benevolence of the Good Spirit of Begashibito Canyon. Bill Carlen used to repair windmills in this isolated place. One day the exhausted Carlen was driving along the area's treacherous roads—little more than rock-strewn paths along the ledges of the canyon—when he dozed off to sleep.

Suddenly he saw a figure in front of his pickup, and Carlen jammed on the brakes and skidded to a stop. He jumped out of the car, fearful that he had killed someone. The figure had vanished. Carlen saw that if he had driven a few feet farther, he would have plunged to his death over a cliff.

The ghost town of Two Guns on the edge of Canyon Diablo has been the target of several evil spirits. Indians claim that the area is cursed and that anyone who settles there is foolish. The first recorded spooky event occurred in June 1878, when a party of Apache raiders attacked the Navajos who lived on the northern edge of the Painted Desert, slaughtering more than fifty men, women, and children. Navajo warriors pursued the Apache assailants on horseback, but they never found them. They simply vanished.

The next day the Apaches attacked another Navajo village, and once again they disappeared into thin air. The Navajo survivors who pursued the Apaches and searched for their tracks in Canyon Diablo heard Apache voices coming out of the ground. They also heard sounds of horses and smelled food cooking. It appeared to the baffled Navajos that their attackers had simply been swallowed up by the earth.

The Navajo pursuers sent back messengers to get help from their village. Then they gathered around a large limestone rock to wait. While waiting, they discovered cracks in the rock that led to a very large cave. It was large enough to hold men and horses. They surrounded the cave and fired into it, and then built a huge fire to block the cave entrance. Before long they heard the Apaches wailing death chants.

After the fire burned out, the Navajos entered the cave and counted forty-two bodies. From that day on, the site has been cursed with evil spirits. Anyone who disturbs the cave suffers serious misfortune.

In 1923, Earl Cundiff filed a 320-acre grazing claim, built a lodge, and became postmaster at Two Guns, which is located near the cave. Many Navajos warned Cundiff to stay away from the cave, but he felt an urge to explore it. Three years later, he was mysteriously shot to death in his post office.

He left his lease to Harry "Indian" Miller, who tried to make the cave a tourist attraction. As with Cundiff, Navajos warned Miller not to go near the cave, but he not only went there, he went in and threw out all the bones, both human and horse. He displayed the Apache skulls in his trading post. Then he hired Hopis to build a pueblo-like building to attract gullible tourists. He added cages of mountain lions and lynx. He survived an attack from the big cats, but his beautiful teenage daughter was killed in a car accident. Finally, Miller gave up the enterprise and left Two Guns.

The curse lived on. In 1971 a fire started at the post's gas station and spread to the underground gasoline storage tank. The trading post, gas station, restaurant, and cafe were totally destroyed in the explosion. Today the cave is blocked by fallen debris. Perhaps the Apache spirits have found peace.

On a mountain in northern Arizona on dark, moonless nights, a large rock glows with the brilliance of a thousands stars. Members of the Hualapai tribe insist it is a warning to stay away; to touch the glowing rock is to die.

The peak it sits on is Music Mountain, a few miles north of Kingman, and it holds a sinister secret despite its lovely name—in fact, many refer to it as Death Trap Mountain. When Lieutenant Joseph C. Ives discovered this peak in 1854, he called it Music Mountain because its strata resembled a sheet of written music. Some claim that a special primeval music whispering on the mountain lures people into Death Trap Gorge, where a glowing blue stone charged with a terrible force deals death to all who touch it. The Hualapais believe an evil god resides in the stone.

In 1895 a party of hunters went into the Cerbat Range in search of bighorn sheep. As they approached Death Trap Mountain and the glowing rock, they startled a sheep, and it plunged blindly into a gorge, falling to its death. The hunters moved towards the gorge to retrieve the sheep, but an ancient Hualapai man stepped into their path and warned them to stay away. He pointed to a pile of bleached bones nearby, saying, "The god in the stone will kill you, too."

The hunters thanked him for saving their lives and gave him gifts of tobacco and food. Then they prevailed upon him to tell the story. While they listened to him, a rattlesnake approached the glowing rock. It slithered up the stone's face, slowly contorted into a horrible coil, raised its evil head, and dropped dead.

According to the storyteller, long ago, beyond the memory of the oldest person in the tribe, a stranger came to the Hualapais. He had brilliant blue eyes and blonde hair, and his body was shriveled and deformed. He had enormous healing talents; often by merely fixing his eyes on a patient, he could cure an ailment. Even wild animals forsook their ferocity and loved him. The Hualapai chief made him a medicine man.

When the chief's son grew to manhood and decided to marry the most beautiful maiden in the tribe, everyone was happy—until the hour of their marriage ceremony came and she was nowhere to be found. A day of joy became a day of sorrow. Finally a toothless old crone told the chief that the blonde stranger had spirited away the bride. They found him near the sacred stone. None would kill him, but the chief ordered him to leave the village at dawn.

The braves followed him out of the village. Before long they realized that he was leading them somewhere. As if he were a magnet, he pulled them. They could neither stop nor retrace their steps. As the sun descended, the stone turned to a lustrous blue and the medicine man invoked the power of the gods. One by one the braves who had been following him dropped dead.

Is the rock still there? Yes. Drunks, liars, and innocent altar boys have seen it. The Hualapais believe it contains a powerful evil force. Should you see the stone, be warned: Don't touch!

The Navajo Reservation is a lonely land where the wind plays its music in the canyon crevices and whispers through the mountain pine forests. Within the Navajo culture, the practice of witchcraft is considered evil, but in recent years, witchcraft and wizardry appear to have become more prevalent on the Big Rez.

A Navajo becomes a witch by violating sacred taboos with such acts as incest, murdering relatives, and handling corpses. When someone becomes a member of the witch society, they take part in frightful initiation ceremonies in a cave, where many more sexual taboos are violated. The ceremonies also involve cannibalism and mutilation of corpses for the preparation of "corpse powder" or "bone darts" that are used in the Shootingway Ceremony, a ritual in which objects are injected from a great distance into the bodies of others, causing illness or harm.

Accusations of witchcraft in Navajo communities may arise from suspicions of breaking taboos, communion with the dead, and assertion of magical power, as well as more common behaviors such as selfishness, belligerence, lying, extramarital affairs, and stealing. Over the years, Navajo communities have levelled charges of practicing witchcraft against those who can't be proven guilty of any specific crime, but who seem to be selected as unworthy of community support—or, in some cases, against those who have chosen to break Navajo custom by not sharing their wealth with the rest of the tribe.

In 1900, Charlie Mitchell, a Navajo headman from Tsaile, expressed bitter hostility towards his clan's powerful medicine men after he returned from a visit to the priests at St. Michael's Mission. He accused the medicine men of being charlatans who used the Shootingway Ceremony. He went on to say that the medicine men would then insist that only through another expensive ritual, the Suckingway Ceremony, could the objects be removed.

Before long, Mitchell's sister dreamed that wizards had bewitched her, and she fell ill with a fever. The priest at St. Michael's cured her with quinine, but the Navajo council insisted on getting to the supernatural roots of the problem, which involved scheduling a Suckingway Ceremony. The woman's husband, who wanted her to have rest and more medical attention, attempted unsuccessfully to halt the ceremony.

The trouble began many years before. Charlie Mitchell and Chee Dodge had met in 1892 at Rough Rock at a meeting that sparked the Black Horse Rebellion. Dodge, one of the few Navajos who spoke English, left his memories on this conflict. Together with a posse of their followers,

Mitchell and Dodge approached Father Anselm at St. Michael's Mission, dragging behind them Charlie McKinley, whom they accused of being an evil shooter. Mitchell, the Tsaile headman, accused McKinley of making a Navajo woman ill by shooting her with an invisible dart or bean. (Darts and beans are used interchangeably in the Shootingway Ceremony.) In spite of a singing ceremony, the woman got worse and died. McKinley had already invited trouble with the tribe when he had boasted of the sweetness of crow meat, which is taboo to eat and so is associated with witchcraft. McKinley became known as Crow Eater.

Mitchell and the other headmen from Tsaile wanted Father Anselm to punish McKinley. Father Anselm neatly sidestepped the issue by claiming that he did not have the authority to punish the man. He suggested that they take their prisoner to the Indian agent at Fort Defiance. The agent declined to become involved in the affair. He sent the headmen home and got even with Father Anselm by putting the prisoner under the protective custody of the friars at St. Michael's.

Father Anselm asked the prisoner to turn over his medicine bundle, which was suspected in the use of witchcraft. McKinley turned over only an insignificant part of the bundle. Eventually McKinley went free and became a practitioner of the Suckingway Ceremony.

Over the years, practitioners of the Suckingway Ceremony formed their own secret society. They often worked in pairs; one would shoot the magic dart into the victim, and the other would wait to be hired by the victim's family to perform the Suckingway. Afterwards they would split the fees for the curing. Practitioners claimed to have removed bone chips, jewelry, cactus spines, charcoal, and human bones during the Suckingway extractions through trickery.

In 1912, a prominent Navajo family sent for McKinley to perform the Suckingway Ceremony for a man named Silversmith, who was also a Shootingway singer, near Lukachukai, an area known as the "wizard's habitat." Several Navajo men suspected that Bineni, McKinley's teacher, shot Silversmith. About fifty Navajos gathered in protest, chanting, "How does he know? What does he know?"

At first McKinley insisted that he knew nothing about the Suckingway Ceremony. Several Navajos, including Charlie Mitchell, Dung Killer,

Slim Curly, Ganado Mucho, and Lefthanded dragged him into the hogan of their sick friend and ordered him to extract the bean before sundown. The terrified McKinley said he had to go home and get his *jish*, or magic bundle, which contained pieces of agate for cutting the victim.

McKinley believed that the offending object would find its way from Silversmith into his own body or his tribesmen would kill him. Either way, he would die. For four days he attempted to extract the objects from Silversmith's body. Mitchell's son told him, "Think very carefully about what you are to do, because Silversmith said that if you have not extracted the dart by tomorrow morning, you are a dead man!"

Fearing for his life, McKinley resorted to chicanery by slipping a few pieces of charcoal in his mouth. He cut Silversmith behind the ear and spit out the charcoal. Fortunately for McKinley, the patient recovered.

Closely interwoven with Shootingway and Suckingway witchery are the Navajo skinwalkers. Navajo skinwalkers were made famous by Tony Hillerman in his novel of the same name. At night, certain people can change into animals such as bear, coyote, and wolf, to wreak havoc on others. Unsolved crimes committed by mere mortals are often blamed on skinwalkers.

Often skinwalkers bewitch the livestock of their intended victims, sometimes assuming the forms of dogs to attack the sheep and horses. Many Navajos tell stories involving skinwalkers on the roof: The family falls asleep at night, only to be awakened when the skinwalker drops "corpse powder" down the chimney.

In 1988, a Coconino County Superior Court jury acquitted a former Northern Arizona University English instructor, George Abney, of first-degree murder in June 1987, on the basis that the victim was ritually murdered by a skinwalker.

The mutilated body of the victim, Sarah Saganitso, had been discovered by co-workers in a rocky area behind the hospital where she worked. The nipple of her left breast had been bitten off, and the prosecution presented forensic evidence that the teeth marks matched those of Abney. The murderer had carved a crescent-moon figure on her breast, where a single animal hair also was found. The prosecution insisted that Abney had confessed to the crime in a telephone call from his mother's house in South Carolina, where he was contemplating a move to China.

Abney's defense presented expert testimony suggesting that Sagan-itso, who was Navajo, had been killed in a manner consistent with Navajo witchcraft involving skinwalkers: carefully placed elements of a broken stick were placed across the victim's neck, and clump of "grave grass" was found next to her pickup. Abney's defense hinted that the victim's boyfriend, a practitioner of the Native American Church, might have committed the murder.

Even today when a powerful dart is shot into a foe's body, it wreaks an evil magic. Even today, witches change into animals at night and cause mayhem for their enemies.

Among the Navajos, those with great power are able to sing into ex-istence a *Chindi* evil spirit, even though the spirit may be in a faraway place. Chindis are avenging angels who take on human or animal form to set things right in the universe and bring down vengeance upon humans who make a mess of things.

For years the Chindi tormented the Long Salts family. In the early 1800s there was a feud in which a member of this family killed Dawn Dancer. Dawn Dancer's spirit became restless and appeared in dreams to various members of the Long Salts family. They hired a medicine man to sing over the murderer's body. After three days and nights of singing, the victim announced that Dawn Dancer had left his dreams.

In return for performing the sing, the medicine man requested four of the choicest sheep from the Long Salts flock, but because the sheep were so far from the Long Salts hogan, two men in the family decided to substitute antelope for the sheep. They thought the medicine man, who was old and blind, would not notice the difference after the animals were butchered.

Long Salts elders, who were unaware of the substitution, escorted the old medicine man home and presented him with the carcasses. A few weeks later a young male member of the Long Salts clan died without any previous illness. Then every few weeks a member of the family would fall ill, waste away, and die. Someone had set a Chindi upon them. The men who cheated the old medicine man grew more frightened. Every day the

Chindi took at least one of them. At last they confessed before the Long Salts clan and the old medicine man.

The medicine man confessed in turn that he became very angry when he detected the substitution, and that he set a Chindi upon the family. Members of the Long Salts begged the old medicine man to call off the spirits. They had not known of the deceit and they fully intended to keep their part of the bargain. The old man was touched by their predicament, but he had to uphold his own honor by not letting himself be cheated. He said, "Today I am tired. Come back in ten days, and you will hear my price."

The Long Salts were disappointed, but they did not dare argue with the old man. On the morning of the tenth day, a delegation of Long Salts waited outside the hogan of the old medicine man. Unfortunately, they found a family in sorrow. The man had died.

Had he recalled the Chindi before he died? When they returned home they had their answer, because several members of the Long Salts family had died, and several more were gravely ill. By 1925 the last three Long Salts family members were ill or crippled and had to be cared for by friends who watched them fade into death.

Finally only Alice Long Salt remained. Hosteen Behegade adopted the young girl, although she, too, was beginning to show signs of becoming lethargic. Behegade was angry that such an awful vengeance had been exacted from so many innocent people, who suffered because of the deceit of two lazy men. Several men offered to conduct sings for free to exorcise the evil Chindi, but within a year, Alice was no better, and Hosteen was heavily in debt from the expenses of caring for her.

Hosteen decided to keep the girl moving constantly so that the Chindi could not finish her off. He attempted to conceal their trail, but one night he heard an owl hoot a warning. The next morning Alice was weak, but they moved on. Hosteen would later claim that the owl had protected them. In the winter of 1928, Hosteen and Alice wandered through a snowstorm into an abandoned hogan near Red Mesa. Alice was suddenly cheerful and seemed to improve in health. Hosteen decided that they could relax, and that night they slept. In the morning Alice Long Salt was dead. The Chindi had returned to complete its one-hundred-year purpose of vengeance.

An animal possessed by a Chindi has dead eyes. If it darts in front of your headlights and its eyes don't glow in the glare, rest assured that it is among the possessed. Start thinking good thoughts, and the beast will probably not hurt you. Still, having crossed the path of a Chindi, it might not be a bad idea to draw a medicine circle around yourself and sing a prayer. It does not need to be a Navajo prayer, but you must have a proper attitude toward the universe. If you have inadvertently desecrated the universe even in some small way, like flinging a beer can out of the car window, the medicine circle may not be able to protect you against the Chindi's energy. If you have thoughts of killing the animal along the road forget it. A bullet will kill the mortal form, but nothing can kill a Chindi.

chapter 10

Military Ghosts

First the Spanish conquistadors came to what is now Arizona, and then the U.S. soldiers came to guard the presidios of western settlers. Between the two groups, many a soldier lad found a lonely grave on the remote desert stretches of our state.

Years ago as sojourners passed by a grave in the desert, it was customary to toss a rock onto it so that the corpse might be protected from coyotes. The pile of rocks on a grave in the rugged mountains near Nogales, Arizona, for many years has protected the body of a Spanish soldier. There is no explanation for what happens to the place at night: A Spanish conquistador in full armor leaves the grave, mounts his steed, and rides into the night.

Many years ago, a group of cowboys relaxed near this site after a hard day's ride on the roundup. The light of stars and a full moon filtered through wispy clouds and lit the beautiful, crisp autumn night.

At first it was just the soft whinny of a horse not their own that caught their attention, but soon it was clear that not just one horse was out there. Perhaps a few rustlers had taken a notion to pass through and help themselves to a bit of prime beef so they could stock their own ranchitos. A shudder rippled through the cattle herd and the cowboys took up their stations.

The sounds of horses running wild came closer and closer, until the men decided to hell with the cattle and scampered behind rocks to protect themselves from the crashing herd. They relaxed when a soldier riding a beautiful white Arabian steed galloped by, but they became alarmed when they noticed that the horse's hooves never touched the ground.

Now, cowboys of all nationalities are apt to see strange things after a drunken night on the town, but these men were stone cold sober, and what they saw of the rider made their blood run cold. He wore the ancient Spanish helmet and a coat of chain-mail. Under the helmet, the ghostly rider's head was nothing but a skull. The cowboys made the sign of the cross when they heard the clinking of fallen coins. The lone rider stopped, turned, and glanced at them one more time before riding on.

The foreman set up an extra watch that night but even so, the men did not sleep well. The next morning their bravery returned. They had never been scared of anything. They went to search for the coins but found none.

Perhaps the man whose ghost appeared to the cowboys was killed in a skirmish with Apaches. Perhaps he had guarded a gold payroll to be carried to the Tubac Presidio. Perhaps the lonely phantom rides only on the anniversary of his death. *Quien sabe?* He still rides. Many have seen him. None have found his gold—yet.

The U.S. military established Camp Lowell to protect the fledgling settlement of Tucson in 1862. At first the camp was located in town along present-day Broadway, but Tucson residents, anxious to show easterners that they had achieved a modicum of civilization, found the soldiers too rowdy, so the army chose a new site at the confluence of the Pantano and Tanque Verde Washes. The post was now assured sufficient water for both horses and men, but troubles with the townsfolk did not diminish. Now the soldiers rode into Tucson, got drunk, and did not go home at night.

Eventually adobe buildings were erected, and Camp Lowell became Fort Lowell. Today Fort Lowell Park welcomes visitors with a museum and the preserved ruins of the old fort, which closed in 1891. Fort Lowell's soldiers may have left, but their ghosts stayed on.

In December of 1900, residents of the Fort Lowell area were disturbed by a new neighbor who took up lodging in the ruins. Almost every night a tall man wearing high boots and the uniform of a soldier would emerge from the adobe walls of Fort Lowell. The residents would fire guns and set their dogs on him, but the dogs refused to get close enough to bite him, and the bullets passed right through him as he dematerialized and disappeared back into the walls.

As the months progressed, more and more reputable citizens reported close encounters with this ghostly soldier. Gun and ammunition dealers did a record business, even though the guns were fired to no avail. The wonderful historic walls of Fort Lowell became riddled with bullet holes.

One night when the soldier got tired of the harassment, he hurled a volley of rocks at his tormentors. On Christmas Eve, he must have felt hungry and lonely because he stole a turkey from a rancher. (The locals shrugged and speculated that perhaps he had shared a good dinner with the other Fort Lowell ghosts. It was difficult to begrudge their ghost a good dinner once a year.)

All was quiet during the early months of 1901, but the soldier reappeared in April. Those who saw the ghost reported that he looked very well after his vacation. So much credibility has been attributed to the Tucson ghost reports that Billy Spear, editor of the *Republican* in Phoenix, put aside his trademark snake stories to give space to the Fort Lowell specter.

Spear reported that one night the ghost appeared in a Fort Lowell house. A man was sitting near his fireplace, enjoying a respite after a hard day's work, when suddenly a great gust of smoke flew out of the fireplace and filled the room. The form of a soldier emerged from the smoke and gazed not unkindly at the frightened rancher. After the rancher bid him welcome in a trembling voice, the soldier vanished back into a cloud of smoke.

The lonely soldier is not the only Fort Lowell ghost. Residents of the Fort Lowell neighborhood report strange goings on—wispy figures, laughter with no one present, doors locking and unlocking of their own accord—in their lovely old houses.

In 1877, Colonel August B. Kautz established Camp Huachuca in the Huachuca Mountains to protect southern Arizona settlers and block Apache escape routes into Mexico. With the construction of permanent buildings, this installation became Fort Huachuca, and it has served the nation in every major war since the 1870s.

In 1913, the Tenth Cavalry of Buffalo Soldiers arrived at Fort Huachuca. Many black soldiers rode with General John J. "Blackjack" Pershing on his punitive expedition into Mexico to stop Pancho Villa's border raids. Ever since, the ghost of a Buffalo Soldier has been seen walking among the rock and wood-frame buildings that house today's garrison offices.

After World War II, Fort Huachuca was declared surplus. The military transferred the abandoned fort to the state of Arizona until the Korean Conflict, when it was reactivated. During the years from 1947 to 1951, when Arizona held the deed to the property, Governors Sidney P. Osborn and Dan E. Garvey used it as a retreat and hunting lodge. A ghost named Charlotte may have moved in during this period. If the governors ever saw her, they never mentioned it. Arizona governors were more circumspect in those days.

Just when Charlotte made her presence known isn't clear; but then, that is often the way with spirits. Charlotte took up residence in the fort's oldest building, the Carleton House. She brought her rocking chair with her. (Rocking chairs appear to be particularly hospitable to spirits.) She rocks in her own space, called Charlotte's Corner, in the Carleton House living room. It is always cold in Charlotte's Corner, no matter what attempts are made to heat it.

The Carleton House was named after Brigadier General James H. Carleton, Commander of the California Column, who retook Tucson for the Union forces during the Civil War. Today the structure is a home for high-ranking officers, but it originally served as a hospital. In 1885 it was found inadequate for that purpose. It has been an officer's mess, schoolhouse, café, and chapel since then.

Stories of Charlotte's ghost started during the time the Carleton House served as a hospital. Charlotte may have been one of the soldiers' wives, and gave birth to a stillborn child before dying herself a few days later. Her ghost is supposed to have told previous residents that she does not believe her child was properly cared for at the hospital before the burial. Charlotte wanders the house in search of her baby, frequently repeating the word *sleep*.

The Carleton House has the usual ghostly occurrences, such as spectral voices, and light switches going on and off by themselves. Residents hear rapping on the door, and when they look, no one is there. Often sleigh bells ring at the dining room door and footsteps are heard in the middle of the night. When Charlotte is having a particularly bad day, pictures fly off the walls and furniture moves of its own accord.

We are not even certain of Charlotte's name. A former resident called the ghost Charlotte because the name has a nice 1800s ring to it. Some younger residents of the house insist that the ghost has told them her name is Barbie.

Children do not seem to be afraid of this ghost, and some have even said that she offers to rock them in her rocking chair. A neighborhood boy has seen a woman walking down a hall wearing a long, white gown with puffy sleeves of a century gone by, her hair coifed in a pompadour style. He claims that she ignored him when he tried to speak to her.

In the Fort Huachuca cemetery, visitors are drawn to two marble slabs set apart from the other graves. They only bear the names Sykes and Rowe, with no other information. These military outcasts lay side by side in dishonor. Their ghosts wander Hangman's Warehouse at night.

Today Hangman's Warehouse is, well, a warehouse. Around the turn of the century, though, this long, narrow, rock building housed army prisoners—AWOL soldiers, renegade Indians, and civilian desperados—and was also the site of executions. It is reputed to be haunted by the last two army men executed there for murder.

On June 9, 1942, a group of soldiers was fooling around in front of the barracks. Private James Rowe jokingly suggested that Private Joseph Shields had stolen a pack of his cigarettes. Shields, not amused, said, "I don't want nobody to accuse me of nothing he didn't see me do."

To put it mildly, Rowe lost his temper. He whipped out a knife and stabbed Shields repeatedly, severing the carotid artery. Shields bled to death within minutes.

Rowe was tried by a general court martial and sentenced to hang. President Franklin Roosevelt and Major General Charles P. Hall approved the sentence. His execution was carried out on November 6. Interment was made without honors in an unassigned portion of the post cemetery.

On June 22, a week after Rowe's trial, Staff Sergeant Jerry Sykes attended a party at the home of First Sergeant Lester Craig and his wife, Hazel, in the community of Fry (now Sierra Vista). Sykes served as the base librarian and was generally known as an all-around nice guy. Hazel Craig had previously dated Sykes, but when Craig got a raise, she dumped Sykes and got married. Sykes still carried a torch for her, for he often lavished her with gifts and gave her a large amount of his paycheck.

That night of June 22, Craig had not yet returned home from the base, and the party started without him. When Hazel and another woman went to the store to buy more liquor, Sykes sneaked into the kitchen and stole a knife. After Hazel returned, Sykes had a drink and went to the bedroom to lie down.

Hazel asked Sykes to take her to Fort Huachuca. Instead, they went to the Blue Moon bar in Fry. On their way back, they got into a violent argument. He pulled the knife in a frenzied rage and stabbed her to death.

Before long, the military authorities found Hazel's body, and people remembered that Sykes had left the house with her. His bloody clothes and the knife were enough for a court-martial conviction. On January 19, 1943, Jerry Sykes was hanged. No one claimed his body, and for several weeks his grave remained open.

Years later a new post commander discovered that Rowe and Sykes were actually buried near the heroes of the Indian Wars. The commander ordered the bodies disinterred and moved to their present locations at the extreme northeast portion of the cemetery.

Several sightings of the ghosts of Sykes and Rowe have been reported. Clearly, these spirits with violent pasts continue to have a difficult time finding peace.

There are quite a few hangars around Arizona, and they are as likely to be haunted as other military structures. Near Tucson, Davis Monthan Air Force Base maintains a large graveyard for mothballed aircraft. Over the years the phantom of a World War II pilot has walked around them, most likely searching for his own plane. According to reports, sometimes when he is there, patrol lights go out and flashlights just won't work. There is no choice but to stand there and watch as the ghost walks right through the security fences and crosses Kolb Road, only to disappear into the night.

The world-famous Champlin Fighter Aircraft Museum in Mesa houses an international collection of fighter planes that have made "Ace"— five or more air-to-air combat victories. From the early open cockpit biplanes of World War I through the jets of Vietnam and Desert Storm, the Champlin Aces are all flyable. Hundreds of photos of ace pilots and other aircraft memorabilia decorate the walls. You could say that the building is filled with the spirit of flight, and you'd be more right than you'd realized.

The German Aviatik D-11 fighter plane at Champlin survived the war, but its pilot evidently did not. He wanders around the museum's Hangar One keeping company with his plane. He opens and closes doors, rearranges the pewter model airplanes, and moves the chairs around to set up for a poker game. He is given to flirting with the female employees. They say they feel his energy, and he likes to blow on the backs of their necks. When the women tell him they aren't afraid of him, he just laughs.

Psychics claim to sense the energy of a fraternity of at least two German spirits among the Champlin Museum aircraft. The pilots have communicated to them that they take great pride in seeing their planes on display.

Very few ghosts have stranger pasts than that of Corporal Hayden J. Johnson, who served at the Kingman Army Air Field near the town of Kingman in World War II. Before coming to Arizona, Johnson was well known in Chicago for his abilities as a Golden Gloves boxer. He had also been a boxing instructor for the Catholic Youth Organization. In the army, he was assigned to the Kingman Army Air Field physical training department and worked as an instructor with the boxing team, even helping the town raise war bond funds with a boxing demonstration in the high school gymnasium.

On March 20 or 21, 1944, Johnson, age twenty-seven, took a military flight on one of the 375 transient planes that served at the Kingman Army Air Field. He planned to spend a furlough with his wife, Adella, and their two sons in Kewanee, Illinois, and soldiers (and their families) were allowed to hitch rides on these planes as space became available. No records or passenger lists appear to have been kept.

On April 25, a rancher, Jesse Williams, discovered Johnson's body in the desert of Hidalgo County, New Mexico, approximately sixteen miles from San Simon, Arizona, and more than five hundred miles from Kingman. The body was still attached to a parachute harness. A chute lay open nearby. No plane had been reported as having crashed in the vicinity of Johnson's body. Did he jump, or was he pushed? And what was the plane doing so far off course?

It was nineteen years after Johnson's death before Adella received any benefits. Her first application was denied on the basis that Johnson's records were not available at the St. Louis Records Center. In 1994, one of Corporal Johnson's sons attempted to research what had happened to his father, with no luck.

Corporal Hayden J. Johnson's body, at least, received proper burial, but his soul seems destined to join the brotherhood of lonely military spirits who wander Arizona's deserts.

Once upon a time, the Frank Luke House in Phoenix hosted visitors renowned in the field of aviation, including Eddie Rickenbacker and Charles Lindbergh. Now, many believe this once-elegant mansion is haunted.

The house was built in 1906 on the edge of the Phoenix city limits (along what is now Monroe Street) by a Southern Pacific Railroad executive. Before long it became part of an ostrich farm operated by C. T. Smith. By 1914, ostrich plumes were in vogue on ladies' hats, and farms around Phoenix raised over eight thousand ostriches.

Frank Luke Sr. purchased the house around 1917. Luke arrived in the Phoenix area around 1880, and married Tillie Liebenow four years later. He served as the Maricopa County assessor and filled a term on the Arizona State Tax Commission. Frank Sr. and Tillie had nine children. In the days the Lukes lived in the house, neighborhood children visited for ice cream socials and skating on the hardwood floors.

In 1944, Phoenix City Councilman Henry Broaderson purchased the house and remodeled it to serve as a boardinghouse, as well as his family's home. One of the residents was the mother of entertainer and songwriter Steve Allen, who became a frequent visitor to the house. The Broadersons were the first to hear strange voices and doors slamming when no people were around.

After the Broadersons moved in 1950, the house changed hands several times, and vandals wreaked destruction on it. Some say that the ghost of a woman who died in a fire in the upstairs kitchen roamed the halls. Another woman, a Luke relative, was also rumored to have died in the upstairs kitchen many years earlier.

The Ronald Duncans lived in the house eight years before selling to Walter Pulaski in 1971. Pulaski believed the house was haunted. He claimed that the temperature remained at a constant seventy-five degrees throughout the house except for one upstairs room, which was cold as death. At night Pulaski and a few of his friends heard tinkling glasses and people laughing as though they were at a farewell party for a soldier boy gone off to war.

After a couple of frightening experiences, Pulaski lived only in the downstairs part of the house. He could put up with the shuffling noises and the clomping of boots on the stairs, but he became terrified when someone entered his bedroom and pulled his hair. He rented the upstairs rooms to a mother and daughter, but they did not stay long, for whenever they touched anything in the cold room, all the lights went out. Pulaski decided it was time to sell when he went up the stairs to investigate the loud noises and felt a rush of cold wind as footsteps marched past him.

Pulaski had trouble selling the house until he advertised that it was haunted. One lady wanted to trade houses. She was tired of her bad-tempered poltergeist and wanted a house with a nicer spirit.

A real estate agent reported an encounter with a weeping woman. She described the slim young woman as having very long hair and wearing an old-fashioned long dress with a ruffled neckline. As soon as her client approached, the woman disappeared.

Many who visited or lived in the Frank Luke House believe its ghosts belong to members of the Luke family, particularly young Frank Luke Jr., one of Frank and Tillie Luke's nine children.

Frank Luke Jr. was Arizona's World War I flying ace. His statue stands in front of the old Capitol Building, and Luke Air Force Base is named for him. He was a handsome, happy-go-lucky lad. At age twenty-one, he fulfilled his patriotic duty by joining America's fledgling air force.

According to the family Bible, during Frank Jr.'s last furlough before being shipped overseas, he planted a large garden of lilies at his parents' home. He flew his first combat mission on September 12, and on September 19 the family received news that Frank had destroyed nine German observation balloons. Frank went missing in action, and on September 29, 1918, the lilies he had planted bloomed for one day in the form of a fuselage, wing, and tail section of an airplane. Tillie Luke brushed away her tears and remarked that something must be wrong with Frank.

Two months later, her worst fears were realized. Frank had been shot down over France and plunged to his death. Although his parents received notice on November 25, two weeks after the Armistice ended World War I, their son had died on September 29—the day the lilies bloomed.

chapter 11

Arizona Bedeviled

There resides in Arizona's Mohave County a group from the Mojave Indian spirit world that begs description, and for the most part defies categorization. It is the *Amatpathenya,* also known as the Mojave leprechauns or the little people.

Endowed with supernatural powers and at least distantly related to the gods, these little people appear out of nowhere to perform useful services for good people, and to confer spiritual powers upon them. They are white-haired and short, standing at about two to four feet in height.

Many members of the Mojave Tribe, which makes its home along the Colorado River Reservation, have their own anecdotes about the Amatpathenya. One Mojave octogenarian described the Amatpathenya he encountered as neither male nor female and resembling a brown-legged rooster, covered in feathers, with an almost human face.

The basic tenet of Mojave religion is that all power and supernatural ability is derived from proper dreaming. Mojaves experience their first dreams in their mothers' wombs. At that time, the soul, or *matkwesa,* of the unborn Mojave is projected back in time to the sacred mountain,

Avikwame, where creation occurred. The deities Matavilya and Mastamho confer such powers as shamanism, bravery, singing, and oratory on a child before it is born. These dreams are forgotten at birth, but they recur when the dreamer enters adolescence and the child's destiny begins to unfold.

Becoming Amatpathenya is a special privilege, for they know everything from the very beginning of creation and are able to see into the future. They take on a human form when they want you to see them, but most of the time they are invisible.

Sometimes the Amatpathenya put people to sleep when they want to teach them things. If you ever wake with new ideas in your head, you might have them to thank. If you have what seems like a dream, you may have had a close encounter with a Mojave elf.

Mojaves have the Amatpathenya, and Mexicans have the *pichilinguis* or *pichilingos*, who make mischief and create nuisances. They are closely related to poltergeists. Mexican parents call their kids pichilinguis when they are driving them nuts.

So, Señor Pistolero, you are thinking you are hot stuff because you just snapped your fingers at the waiter and that young señorita is looking at you with soft, dreamy eyes. Suddenly a cow pie flies through the window and lands right on top of your tamales. Then a pile of burro droppings lands in your beer. Did you notice the waiter laughing at the work of the pichilinguis?

If you have been bragging and bragging about how much milk your cow gives and the next morning she is "udderly" dry, it's likely the pichilinguis have milked her and let all that milk run down the road. If your favorite saint has been tossed headfirst down a well, guess who?

At night someone pulls the mosquito netting off you, and in the morning you discover that the insects have been feasting on the most tender parts of your body. You go into the chicken coop and are greeted by a barrage of eggs and giggles. Blame the pichilinguis.

Pichilinguis are great at spreading gossip among animals. If you wondered why your usually gentle horse dumped you in the ditch, now you know. The pichilinguis told him that you are short changing his oats because you squandered your dinero on Rosie in the cantina.

Arizonans are most fortunate to share our state with a troll. Many think Hank the Winslow Troll is evil, but it just may be that he is lonely. After all, he is the only one of his kind in the state. Trolls are related to ancient Icelandic ogres; just how one happened to get under an Arizona bridge defies imagination.

As you may remember from the story of the Billy Goats Gruff, trolls have the annoying habit of pulling folks under water. Hank is no exception. Near the Clear Creek Bridge, about six miles southeast of Winslow, he's been known to pull lovers' in parked cars into the reservoir. One night he gave chase to a high school track athlete. The kid broke all records, but no one was there to officially time him. In Winslow, everybody knows that Hank will get you if you go near the bridge.

Teenagers drinking beer by the reservoir after a high school football game heard Hank's low gurgling sounds and saw bubbles on the water. They waited and watched for awhile, and then *kaploosh!* he got someone—but they didn't see who. Their group was all accounted for, so Hank's victim must have been a stranger. Nevertheless, just to be on the safe side, they decided that maybe they'd better hightail it home.

Those who have seen Hank from the opposite bank say he is covered with dark, slimy feathers and has a flat, roughly egg-shaped head that is disproportionately large. He usually crawls along on all fours, but when he stands up, he is about nine feet tall.

If you go to find Hank, you may rendezvous with him, or you may just see his bubbles in the water at midnight. Either way, be careful. He's waiting for you.

Chupacapras, also known as the hell monkeys from beyond, are the new ghouls on the Arizona block. Until recently, chupacapras stayed south of the border, sucking the blood of forty-six beasts and people in fourteen Mexican states. They're originally from Puerto Rico, where they sucked dead twenty parakeets and a stuffed teddy bear, and have been held responsible for several waves of bloody terror there.

Chupacapras flew in to Tucson around June 1996 without so much as showing their green cards or buying trinkets in Nogales first—they went right to work sucking blood out of goats, geese, cattle, and horses. Old-time Tucsonans say that the chupacapra invasion is nothing new at all. They recall stories of a goat-sucker who came up from Nogales in the 1950s. The creature, which looked like a giant kangaroo, sneaked up behind people at night for a taste of their blood, and left the remains of flocks of chickens across Arizona before disappearing—temporarily. During the 1970s the evil 'roos were spotted as far north as the cornfields of Nebraska and the southern tip of Tennessee, and also appeared in San Antonio, Miami, New York City, and even Moscow, Russia. They left mutilated cattle and dogs in their wake.

In the latest round of visits, a critter hopped through an open window at one Tucson home and sat on top of a young boy. The boy's aunt identified the footprints as those of a chupacapra. Tucson police said they belonged to the child, but who do they think they are to argue with a little boy's ghost-busting auntie? On its way out, the creature left a rancid piece of meat on the windowsill.

At a ranch near Oracle a young boy heard the door of an outhouse creak, and then a tall, kangaroo-like creature peered around the edge of the door and beckoned him to come forward. The frightened boy took the safe course and ran like hell.

One Tucson woman, accused of having an illicit love affair, said a chupacapra was to blame for her hickey.

The Puerto Rican origins of the chupacapra stories are murky, but are believed to have been derived from indigenous legends combined with European stories about a goat-sucker. In Spanish, *chupacapra* means "goat-sucker." (Humor writer Dave Barry claims the word is Puerto Rican for lawyer.) Sightings have been sketchy, but chupacapras are variously believed to have the features of a vampire, a kangaroo, a turkey, with a skosh of armadillo. Some say the creature looks like E.T. on a bad hair day.

The monster that first landed at a small rise off Tucson's Tanque Verde Road was described as having an eight-foot wingspan and a two-foot beak. It stood about five feet tall and looked kind of furry, with a crest of spikes starting at its forehead and running down its back. It had a long tube in its mouth for sucking its victims' blood. It left behind a revolting stench; kids say it smells like a wet dog. One Tucson family that had a firsthand experience with the creature described it as winged with big red eyes, powerful hind legs, skimpy forelegs, pointy nose and ears, and a gray hide covered with quills and lots of wrinkles. Well, you get the picture.

A Tucson scientist has postulated that chupacapras may in fact be mutant gryphons, the four-legged raptors immortalized in heraldic crests and coats of arms. Others believe they're just really big birds, which makes sense, since Arizona has always been on the cutting edge of odd birds. (More evidence for the bird theory: Scientists have grouped birds such as nightjars and poorwills into the species *caprimulgida,* or goatsuckers.) Some say they are in fact the thunderbirds. Still others believe the creatures are pterodactyls that survived in a remote stretch of the Andes until they migrated to Puerto Rico and the mainland United States.

The Thunderbird, part of Native American lore, is a huge *rara avis* that generates lightning with its eyes and causes thunder claps by flapping its massive wings. A pterodactyl, sometimes referred to as the Thunderbird, appeared to Tombstone cowboys as early as 1890.

Two cowboys saw a giant flying bird, which they shot and killed with their rifles. With their two horses they managed to drag the carcass, about the size of a modern single-engine Cessna plane, into town. The *Tombstone Epitaph* noted on April 26, 1890, that the bird had a head about eight feet long. However, it had no feathers, just a transparent membrane that was easily pierced by a bullet.

Some say the cowboys' spooked horses refused to have anything to do with the giant bird, so the pair walked into town empty handed except for their bizarre story. Over the years the story grew—and so did the bird. In 1953, the bird appeared in a rip-snortin' tale in *Saga* as the "Monster Bird That Carried Off Human Beings," in which the bird supposedly snatched a heckler who scoffed at its existence. A picture accompanied the story: eight cowboys standing behind a spooky avian corpse, its mighty wingspan unfurled. Though the photo was clearly a fake, before long, people's vague memories had them believing that the story was printed in esteemed publications such as *National Geographic.*

In 1990 a twenty-one-year-old Mesa woman awoke to find half of one of her ears missing, and a large reptile was flying out of her window. Mesa police said her behavior was "not logical."

Along the Mexico-U.S. border, enterprising hucksters sell a variety of animal skeletons as remains of baby chupacapras. Food vendors sell a blood-red concoction that is supposed to have aphrodisiac essence of chupacapras, as well as chupa sandwiches, drenched in salsa and filled with a mystery meat—probably goat.

I cannot tell you exactly where you can find the Sacred Serpent, but I do know that he has been seen in wells and caves all over Arizona. Tucson's Sacred Serpent inhabits a well in the old part of town, and legend has it that if he dies, the city's water supply will dry up and everyone will either die of thirst or have to drink Central Arizona Project (CAP) water.

The Sacred Serpent sparkles with brilliant green scales and red ruby eyes. He is at least thirty feet long and weighs well over two hundred pounds. Most people would run as far as possible from such a creature, but lore has it that if his long red tongue kisses your lips, you will be endowed with great wisdom. Of course, if his poisonous fangs sink into your flesh, then you have met the essence of evil and you will die an excruciating death.

Many believe that the Aztec god, Quetzalcoatl, was reincarnated as the Emperor Montezuma, and that since the 1520 conquest of Mexico by Hernán Cortés, Montezuma's spirit has roamed the Americas. It is believed that he wields even greater power now because the Sacred Serpent accompanies him. In less than a century Montezuma and his Sacred Serpent have become thoroughly incorporated in North American lore. Greedy treasure hunters, searching for the great caches of gold and precious jewels that Montezuma is supposed to have hidden in Arizona caves, have been struck down by lightning—Montezuma's sacred fire. Of course, the legends have done nothing to discourage the looting of old churches and sacred Indian burial grounds.

Native American healers say they met the Sacred Serpent on a vision quest. They purified themselves in a sweat lodge and fasted for several days, and then the Sacred Serpent beckoned them into its cave and swayed before them with wide-open jaws. They stuck their heads into the serpent's jaws without fear, as a supreme demonstration of faith, and received a talent for healing. I do not recommend that you try this at home.

The Sacred Serpent has been invoked to punish evil men such as White Mountains trading post operator Malcolm Reeves. For the most part, early traders were honest and fair with their Indian clients. If they were lucky, those who were not trustworthy simply found that their income dwindled as the locals took their business elsewhere. Known to cheat his Apache clientele in the 1870s by selling pawn before the elapsed time and believed to abuse young Apache girls, Malcom Reeves was not so lucky.

A medicine man went deep into the mountains where he fasted, chanting and invoking the spirit of Montezuma and the Sacred Serpent. After nine days without food or water, the shaman was approached by Montezuma, who stood almost seven feet tall and was clothed in a robe covered with the brilliant feathers of the copper-tailed trogon, the blue cotinga, and the green Quetzalcoatl. He wore a gold headdress that almost blinded the shaman with its brilliance. Behind him, a giant green serpent swayed and slithered.

The snake went to the trading post and lay in wait until Reeves came outside. Then the Sacred Serpent gave a mighty shake of its rattles and sank its fangs into the trader's leg. Reeves emitted an ungodly shriek before descending into the netherworld.

Malcolm Reeves's trading post is gone, but those who have camped in the area at night have heard the screams and roars of someone in terrible pain. During the day, hikers have seen the shimmering image of a man dressed like a coarse mountaineer stalking them. He beckons for them to wait. Occasionally an Apache shaman appears, followed by a giant serpent, and tells good folk to leave the evil area. Ignore his warning at your own risk.

chapter 12

La Llorona

"It was a dark and stormy night"—an unremarkable opening for a story, except that such a night is a rarity in southern Arizona deserts. When such a night roars across the land, water overflows the banks of many typically dry riverbeds, including the Santa Cruz. On such a night, La Llorona prowls the land.

One dark and stormy night many years ago, Tomás, Ricardo, and Harry spent several hours in a Tucson cantina exchanging stories about the women they had charmed. Tomás, being the oldest, related the longest, most vivid, most deceptive descriptions, even though he knew full well the reality of his life: When he got home and pounded on the door to be let in, his Rosa would probably turn over in bed and snore, pretending to sleep. The middle-aged Ricardo gamely responded with brilliant, captivating prevarications of his own. Harry, the youngest and just married, listened and said nothing.

Tomás guzzled fiery mescal. Ricardo, more genteel, quaffed tequila with salt and lime. Young Harry sipped his beer. Cantina patrons cheered when Tomás took the last swig from the bottle of mescal and proved his manhood by consuming the worm at the bottom.

Finally the bartender broke up the camaraderie and threw everyone out so he could go home. Plaintive violin music wafted through the cloudy night air, recalling an unrequited love affair between a beautiful poor girl and her wealthy, upper-class lover. Suddenly all three men shivered as a chill passed over them. (Remember, this is Tucson in the summertime.)

"What was that?" Harry asked.

"Nothing, nothing," the others replied. They shuddered as they staggered along the banks of the Santa Cruz.

A cry came out of the darkness: "Ay! Ay! Ay!"

"Did you hear that?" Harry asked.

Tomás and Ricardo responded in unison, "No! I heard nothing."

The cry came again, louder: "Ay! Ay! Ayee-e-e-e-e!" The men trembled and crossed themselves. Then again, louder still: "Ay! Ay! Ayee-e-e-e-e-e-e! *Mis hijos!*" At the Spanish words for "my sons," the men tried to run, but their knees buckled and their legs wobbled.

Tomás muttered, "By the Holy Virgin, I will never drink anything stronger than water again."

Ricardo stammered, "B-B-B-B-B-B-Blessed M-M-M-M-Mother, I will go to Mass every Sunday."

Harry vowed, "I will never touch another drop of liquor, and I will go to church every Sunday." He paused, and then added, "And I will have nothing more to do with you two old *borrachos*."

Thunder split the heavens, and in the brief streak of lightning that followed, the men saw a shadowy form, wrapped in a long black robe, emerge along the riverbank. The men froze in their tracks at the edge of the bridge as the tall wraith came towards them, but then they saw there was nothing to fear. Tomás said, "It is only a beautiful young woman."

They had relaxed too soon, for the apparition went right past the bridge and floated over the river. The three compadres heaved a collective sigh of relief when she floated up a hill and disappeared at the top.

A few moments later, the figure reappeared, beckoning the men to come closer, and they found they were compelled to do as she asked. When they got within a few feet of her, she pulled back her hood. Tomás, Ricardo, and Harry opened their mouths to scream, but no sound came out. They gazed into the deep, hollow sockets of her skull and knew they were staring into the eyes of death. The woman raised a hand with long claws and touched Tomás on his cheek. All three men spun around and ran away as fast as possible, her hideous screams piercing their souls and echoing in their pounding heads.

When the sun came up, the screams had stopped and the men had rested. Tomás gingerly felt his cheek and discovered a painful burn left by the touch of La Llorona.

For awhile, Tomás, Ricardo, and Harry argued about whether they should quit drinking altogether or return to the cantina and never stop drinking. Tomás leaned toward the former, while Ricardo argued for the latter. All Harry said was, *"Ay, dios mio!"*

La Llorona was first seen on a moonlit night in 1550 wandering the streets of Mexico City dressed in white. She was believed to be the ghost of a girl named Malinche, who was sold to the Aztec royal family by her parents just after her birth. She grew up and fell in love with the Spanish Conquistador Hernán Cortés, but Cortés deserted her for a Spanish woman. Malinche went insane and drowned his child. Her ghost, *La Llorona*, "the weeping woman," still searches the streets of Mexico City for her child, keening her anguished, blood-curdling screams before disappearing into a lake.

The story of Malinche finds its roots in the Aztec legends of Cihuacohuatl, the snake woman; Teoyaominiqui, who cared for dead souls; and, Quilaztli, who bore twins. Every night these three goddesses floated around the skies wrapped in white shrouds. Each carried a cradle on her shoulders. They shrieked in despair for their lost children, whom they had sacrificed to the rain god, Tlaloc. Their tears showered down on the parched earth.

There are countless versions of La Llorona. In most, La Llorona is a killer who committed the unpardonable, heinous crime of infanticide, though some believe her baby (or babies) died by accident or from neglect. Some say she drowned her children to spite an unfaithful husband. Some say she was a prostitute who drowned the many children resulting from her promiscuity. Some even say that she was born a twin, and she and her sister looked so much alike that the priest baptized the sister twice and missed La Llorona altogether. She died a lost soul and to this day cannot enter heaven.

Although she traditionally has made appearances in Mexico, Arizona, Texas, New Mexico, and the Philippines, Hispanic workers have migrated north from Mexico to the steel mills in recent years, and La Llorona has ventured as far afield as Indiana. In all regions she hovers in the air over trees, roofs, and riverbanks, but always near water, and especially when the wind blows hard. She prefers lakes and rivers, but in Arizona, ravines, ditches, irrigation canals, Tucson's Stone Avenue underpass, and even dry riverbeds will do. La Llorona knows that water flows underground in the dry riverbeds.

Coincidentally (or maybe not so coincidentally) these places are also good parking spots for young lovers ignoring their curfews. Teenagers have always liked to take the family car out to spots where they can find warm love and cool liquor. The boys claim they are not scared of La Llorona, and the girls get suckered into snuggling just a little closer.

There are nearly as many variations on the details of La Llorona's appearance as there are on her origins. Some see her as a beautiful, young, raven-haired woman, enshrouded in a white cloak, while others perceive a crippled old woman with long white hair and a black cape. Her fingernails usually glisten like knives in the starlight, and in nearly all cases, she pierces the night with cries for her lost children.

It's not surprising that descriptions of La Llorona vary; one cannot expect perfect details from those who have had encounters with the other side. After all, any policeman will tell you that there are as many versions of a fender bender as there are observers. No matter which description of her you believe, remember this: To see her is to be full of fear; to speak to her is to be driven mad; to feel her cold breath, or to touch her is to die.

Around 1910, Don Rafael Urquidez worked for the Southern Pacific Railroad of Mexico. He and his family kept odd hours, because his shift ended around midnight, and when he got home his wife would feed him supper while he played with his little daughter, Dolores. On one of these late nights the family heard a terrible, inhuman wail. In the morning they found a baby, partially devoured by animals, in a nearby arroyo. The baby's parents were never found. For some time the wailing at night continued.

Dolores grew up to be Señora Dolores Urquidez de Garcia, and she had a son named Alex who never forgot his mother's encounter with La Llorona. Every Sunday in the 1930s and 1940s, the families of Alex Garcia and Walter Laos would gather to share an abundance of food and an even bigger abundance of stories. As twilight fell, the men would gather the children and tell them tales of La Llorona to make them behave:

> One night little Pablito tarried too long at the Santa Cruz River. After the summer monsoons, such interesting things washed ashore: a broken bicycle wheel, pretty colored beads, a shoe, and finally something that wiggled when he touched it. For a while Pablito played with the harmless little garden snake, watching innocently as the sun changed its brilliant colors and descended behind the mountains. Then he wound the little snake around his arm and walked toward home. Too late! La Llorona stepped out of the shadows and blocked his path. She had long black hair, and her eye sockets were on fire. She gracefully started to turn away, but then she let out her hideous cry and snatched Pablito with her long fingernails. No more Pablito.

Oftentimes throughout the week that followed, the children would be reminded, "Be good or La Llorona will get you!" or "Don't cry! La Llorona will get you!"

In many Arizona families children are told of La Llorona to scare them away from water. Some mothers just talk about her with each other in low voices, hoping the children will eavesdrop and find the stories more frightening than direct warnings.

It is said that one night a Tucson widow's son drowned while playing near the overflowing Santa Cruz River. The insane, grieving mother now tries to kidnap children. Her fingerprints have been found on windows near Main and Simpson Streets; screens have been torn where she has tried to enter homes. It's no wonder that Tucson mothers always check to make certain their children are properly tucked in at night. If La Llorona finds them, she will take them for herself.

A typical La Llorona encounter: One night a couple of honeymooners from Nogales saw La Llorona kneeling in the middle of a road next to the Santa Cruz. She begged them, "Please help me look for my children. You will be very sorry if you do not help me." The terrified newlyweds drove right through her. La Llorona appeared to the couple two more times, but each time, they sped off. By morning the honeymooners had died. They should have helped La Llorona.

This story may be typical, but not all encounters with La Llorona are brushes with evil. Years ago La Llorona haunted one Tucson neighborhood for a couple of weeks, and terrified neighbors began to band together at night for safety's sake. It turned out to be a ploy by a clever thief with a costume and an uncanny imitation of the ghost's wail. When all the residents huddled together at night, the criminal was free to rob the empty houses. Locals eventually caught on, and someone even took a potshot at him before he got away. The wailing and thievery stopped. A few days later, garbage collectors found the discarded costume.

Tucsonans are also known to attribute *good* luck to La Llorona's presence. The Tucson farm of Baffert and Leon got its start when the founders saw La Llorona standing in their pig sty. They dug under the sty and discovered enough money to set themselves up in the pork business.

Three times a Tucson woodchopper saw La Llorona standing under the same tree. One day he got up enough courage to dig under it, but when he struck a hard object, he got scared and fled. Later he told his brother about it. The brother said nothing but dug in the same spot and uncovered twenty-five thousand dollars in gold. A few days later the wealthy brother died and left his estate to the poor woodchopper.

Sometimes La Llorona just wants to teach a lesson in good manners. One night Diego and Julio had a hurtful argument with their father. They took his wagon and his best horse and set out for town. Just as they turned at the top of a ridge, a woman appeared between them on the wagon seat.

The terrified boys felt her presence as much as they saw her. She wore the black shroud of the dead. A veil hung over her face and partially obscured her long silver earrings. They tried to talk to her, but no words came out of their dry throats. Julio kept driving the horses for fear that if he stopped, something terrible would happen.

Just as they neared the bright lights of the town's cantinas, the woman spoke: "I shall visit you again someday when you argue with your father."

She disappeared from the wagon and floated off toward the cemetery. The terrified boys sat very still for awhile. Then in the distance near the river they heard "Ay! Ay! Ayee-e-e-e-e-e-e-e-e! *Mis hijos!*" They turned around and drove home as fast as possible. From then on, whenever they were inclined to be disrespectful to their father, they remembered La Llorona.

In Mexico and southern Arizona, La Llorona may be the poor maiden Luisa, who slept with a high-born lad and met with tragedy. Luisa lived in an impoverished neighborhood in a dilapidated shack with a roof that leaked when it rained, and though she had neither family nor worldly wealth, she did possess great beauty and charm.

As Luisa grew older, she realized that because of her poor standing she would never marry into money, so she chose instead to be the illicit lover of a young man from a rich family. He set her up in a nicely furnished love nest, and there she had three lovely babies. Luisa was greatly happy, and she believed her lover to feel the same. Perhaps he *was* content—for a little while.

Then his family introduced him to a beautiful woman of high social standing and great wealth. They urged him to break off his dalliance with Luisa, and so he did. He told her that he was about to marry, and that he would not be seeing her anymore. In her despair, she flew into a rage and drove him from her *casita.*

On the day of the wedding, the broken-hearted Luisa sat in the back pew of the cathedral, hiding her face behind a black *rebozo.* She watched as the marriage procession walked to the home of the bride. Her tears flowed when she saw that her lover looked at his new wife with the same tenderness that he had once reserved for her. She knew that he no longer loved her.

Wild with grief, Luisa left the wedding and returned to her home, where her three babies slept. She found a dagger and plunged it into the tiny heart of each child. Then, spattered with blood, she realized that she had committed a terrible abomination. Soon the police arrived and took her away. After Luisa's trial, the village watched her execution: strangulation with a spiked collar.

It is said that when Luisa approached the pearly gates, God asked her, "Where are your children?" She responded with a lie, saying that they had gotten lost, and the Almighty told her, "Then you must find them. Until you find them you cannot enter heaven." Checking all her options, Luisa then discovered that the devil imposed the same restrictions on her entry into hell. Her spirit is now condemned to wander the lonely nights in search of her children, who float in limbo between heaven and hell. Her ghost still appears on ranches near her village, her arms folded, as if to cradle a baby, in anticipation of finding her child.

In one twist on the story of the impoverished Luisa, La Llorona is a wealthy Spanish lady who fell in love with a poor man. Though her parents refused to let them marry, the couple had two children. A rich man then proposed to La Llorona, and her mother told her to hide the children. She killed them instead.

Along the Arizona-Mexico border, La Llorona is the ghost of María, who was once the most beautiful girl in the town of Nogales. María was unusually tall with flowing black hair that reached her ankles. Her skin glowed like alabaster, and she had brown eyes that were like dreamy pools. She was treated spitefully by jealous girls, and the boys were so enraptured with her beauty that they were afraid to speak to her for fear she would reject them.

One day a tall, dark, handsome stranger rode into town on a noble white steed. In one of the town's cantinas he treated locals to lots of drinks and graciously lost oodles of money gambling. After awhile, he stood up and said, "I have become bored. I must move on."

Needless to say, the men did not want him to leave. They pleaded, "Wait! There is someone you must see. We have the most beautiful girl in the world right here in Nogales."

The skeptical stranger shrugged. "What could be the harm of waiting a few more hours?" he asked. Indeed, he wondered what beauty could be found in this harsh desert land of dust and drought. He needed the sweetness of a lovely woman to mitigate his maddening wanderlust.

The stranger cleaned up, trimmed his handsome moustache, put on his fine riding clothes and snowy white sombrero, and rode out to the girl's hacienda. To his surprise he discovered that not only was María the most beautiful girl in the world, she also had a soft, gentle manner. That very day, the stranger fell on his knees and begged her to marry him. María's parents had been worried that they would not be able to provide adequately for their daughter, so they agreed to the union immediately.

After the marriage, María bore a handsome, intelligent son. She kept a clean house, prepared delicious meals, and never scolded her husband for drinking and gambling. Then, just as suddenly as he had arrived, the handsome stranger left, never to return. Night after night, María lit candles, prayed, and cried herself to sleep. Before long, she went crazy.

One stormy night the Santa Cruz flooded with torrential monsoons. María grabbed her son and dashed out the door just as the wind and rain brought down their home. With all her strength, she hurled her child into the rushing waters of the river. She gasped as her son's tiny body turned into that of a fish. In a moment of lucidity, María perceived the evil of her deed and cried out to the heavens, "Ay! Ay! Ayee-e-e-e-e-e-e-e! *Mi hijos!*"

To this day, people of excellent repute see La Llorona scooping fish out of the Santa Cruz River in hopes that one will turn back into her son. There are those wretched doubters who argue that the river has never had fish in it, but they are best ignored.

In Williams La Llorona appears as an old woman enshrouded in a flowing, pale blue gown. She carries a candle to light her way along the Santa Fe Dam, and she never leaves any footprints. Williams residents may have the privilege of seeing her as just a light or a glow in the woods.

In Yuma La Llorona has been seen wandering around Sanguinetti Park, where, the story goes, she gave birth to a child out of wedlock. Ostracized by her family and friends, she waited until the Colorado River had risen very high and threw her baby into the raging waters. Then she jumped in herself. Another story says that she permitted her children to swim in the canals that feed off the Colorado; one night the river overflowed, and the children drowned. Yuma residents have seen her at the canal off the

Sixteenth Street hill. Others swear that she may be found on the night of a full moon at the All American Canal. High school students swear she can be found at Prison Hill, and to be cool they go there after football games, wait for her, and then run like hell. Although some Yuma residents have seen her, many more have heard her cry, which they describe as something between a coyote's howl and the ululations of an otherworldly creature.

In Flagstaff, La Llorona soars over the rooftop of her old house, where she chopped up her children with an axe. At night ghost watchers see a demented blue figure floating horizontally around the chimney, axe in hand, shrieking for her poor children.

Texans seem to lose their fear of La Llorona after hearing her scream for the first time; then they become addicted to the "Ay! Ay! Ayee-e-e-e-e-e-e-e! *Mis hijos!*" To alleviate their cravings, they can call her at an 800 number. She also has over eight hundred sites on the Internet.

La Llorona's ghost is unique in that she moves from place to place. Usually, self-respecting ghosts hang around the site of their violence. La Llorona, on the other hand, has traveled with her misery from Mexico City to Gary, Indiana, from Los Angeles to New Mexico. She's been wandering the land for more than four centuries.

The sorrowful supplications of La Llorona can never be mistaken for anything of an earthly nature. If one night you should decide to investigate a figure of a weeping woman walking along the river and you get too close, be careful. Remember what happened to Tomás, Ricardo, and Harry. When pitiful wails of a supernatural nature give you goosebumps and make your hair stand on end, maybe you had better hurry home. That is, if it's not too late.

chapter 13

The Blue Nun

One of the most lovely, luminous spirits in Arizona's history is the Blue Nun. Sister Mary of Agreda instructed Native Americans in Texas, New Mexico, Colorado, and Arizona in the Christian faith hundreds of years ago. Now she occupies a special place in the Indian stories of the region, and is variously known as Mary of Agreda, Sister Mary, the Blue Nun, the Lady in Blue, and La Señora Azul. She still appears in the American Southwest to perform miracles for the faithful.

Sister Mary, always cloaked in the blue robe of the Poor Clares (a Franciscan order for women), visited Native peoples in America's Southwest almost one hundred years before Spaniards explored these lands—yet she never left Spain, where she was born. She was a bilocator mystic.

As explained by experts, bilocators remain in one place physically, while transporting their spirits to another part of the world during a process known as teleportation. Certain experts believe that bilocators can also transport their physical bodies anywhere they want. All of us have had moments when we felt like we had to be two places at once, and bilocators really do just that.

Sister Mary may have spoken in her own tongue while the listeners heard her words in their language. Perhaps she spoke a mysterious universal language that has been lost in the mists of antiquity. Still another possiblity holds that during her spiritual trances, the Blue Nun spoke in the Pentecostal tongues of the Bible known as glossolalia.

When Spanish missionaries arrived in the Southwest, they learned of Sister Mary from the leaders of Indian tribes. New Mexico and Texas tribal elders said, "She came down from the hills and spoke to us in our language," and the people listened to her reverently. Arizona Indians also acknowledged visits by the Blue Nun, but claimed that they could not understand her, and actually, they didn't want her around. When they tried to shoot her with arrows, she became quite provoked and scolded them.

When arrows struck her, angels crowned her with the crown of martyrdom. Although ill-treated, she did not go quietly. Sister Mary scared the bejammers out of her tormenters, when she continued to descend upon them several times and rose to the heavens, exhorting them to accept the true faith. Sprits have an advantage in that human weapons cannot destroy them.

Mary Coronel, born April 2, 1602, to Francisco and Catalina Coronel, grew up in the village of Agreda, on the border of Aragon and Castile. Mary's father, a Spanish nobleman, had inherited the largest castle in the area. Her mother, Catalina of Arana, gave birth to eleven children, seven of whom died in infancy. Francisco had a hot temper, and Catalina possessed a sharp tongue. Both were religious and strict with their children.

The entire Coronel family presented a faithful but not altogether normal household. Neighbors reported that in Francisco's daily devotions, held from three to six each morning, he usually flagellated himself while exhorting God to save his soul. During Catalina's morning prayers, she shrouded herself in a Franciscan habit and clutched a skull while simulating death on a cross. She used a variety of objects to draw blood as penance. She was also known to spend her household money on her favorite charities, never minding that the family went hungry.

Although Mary was born into the world of Cervantes, Calderon de la Barca, Ignacio de Loyola, and the famous mystic, St. Teresa de Avila, her entire library likely consisted of only the Bible and a prayer book. She never revealed exactly how she learned to read and write, but she insisted that God taught her. She showed a precocious penchant for religious life and an intellect for the interpretation of Scripture.

As soon as Mary could talk, she began conversing with what her parents considered imaginary playmates. This is not unusual for children to do, but by Mary's fourth birthday, she insisted that she was hearing the voice of God. Her terrified parents tried to suppress these notions. The less they believed her, the more little Mary withdrew into her own world.

At age eight, Mary informed her parents that she intended to join a convent. They asked her to wait, and for four years she did, but at age twelve she was just as insistent. Her parents turned her over to the Sisters of Teresa in nearby Tarrazona. They thought the privations of a convent life would dispel her thoughts of heavenly visitors. The visits from God only intensified.

Then one morning in 1615, Mary's mother received a vision during her prayers. She told her priest that the voice commanded that the entire family—including Mary, her sister, two brothers, and parents—enter a religious order. Catalina's confessor, Father Juan de Torrecilla, confirmed that he, too, had the same vision. He reminded Catalina of Christ's words to "sell all that thou has and give it to the poor."

The vision caused a domestic explosion, pitting Francisco against Catalina, her daughters, and the visions and voices. Although Francisco was also very religious, he was sixty, suffered from ulcers, and had no desire to break up his family and be evicted from his estate in this fashion.

Most of Agreda agreed with Francisco. The peasant population was heartily sick and tired of having to support a growing number of religious orders. Spain was economically deprived, and the general population was expected to provide housing and food for a demanding clergy. Moreover, the country appeared to have an abundance of overwrought, hysterical nuns claiming to be recipients of secrets from Christ or his holy mother.

Around 1618, three years after Catalina's vision, she, Mary, and the priest convinced Francisco that he was committing a grievous sin by disobeying God's orders. He reluctantly agreed to convert his ancestral castle into a convent for the Order of the Poor Clares of Saint Francis. Catalina insisted that the Order of the Poor Clares should be governed by the strict rules of the Discalced (unshod) Conceptionists, who were totally devoted to the service of the Virgin Mary.

Catalina and the Coronel daughters entered this convent, and Francisco and the Coronel sons trudged off to a Franciscan monastery. During the remaining seven years of his life, Francisco visited the convent only to join Catalina in renouncing their wedding vows, and to witness Catalina and the girls, Mary and Jeronima, take their vows as nuns. Francisco's ulcers disappeared with his money.

Sister Mary suffered from poor health throughout her life. Nevertheless, she did penance by wearing a coat of mail with a girdle of spiked rings, chains, and fetters against her skin. Even against her confessor's admonitions, she participated in long, debilitating fasts. Though her parents had founded her order, Sister Mary suffered ostracism and physical torment from the other nuns. They found her extreme piety irritating, her trances disturbing, and her penances insane. They, too, had visions from Christ, and who did she think she was, anyway?

In her own writings, Mary admitted to being tempted by impure thoughts from an early age. The devil took advantage of these weak moments to visit her in the form of an incubus. (Go ahead, look it up.) Ghosts and apparitions of fierce creatures besieged her during her prayers. Unclean fiends attempted to corrupt her with impure words and obscene images. Throughout her teenage years, Sister Mary remained silent in her misery and met hostility with forgiveness. She responded to visits from the devil with more fasting, prayers, and self-flagellation.

At age seventeen, Sister Mary's visions took on a new dimension. Multitudes of semi-naked pagans living and dying on a faraway desert without ever hearing about the true faith appeared before her in dreams. The more she prayed, the more these visions oppressed her. Then Christ appeared to her in a dream, and she learned that he was particularly well disposed toward seeing her minister to the Native tribes of what would become the Southwestern United States. However, nuns were forbidden from missionary efforts, which were still the privilege of priests. If Mary would carry out her mission, Christ would have to show her another course of action.

In 1620 during Whitsuntide communion prayers, the congregation gasped at the way Sister Mary's appearance had changed in her two years in the convent. Even the half-witted beggar at the gate remarked that a dazzling blue light engulfed Mary's body, and her face bore the expression of heavenly rapture. Then she levitated about four feet off the ground, and her dark countenance transformed into an alabaster radiance not unlike that of the saints. From that time on, church members remarked that wherever she went, Sister Mary left behind a delicious, celestial perfume.

Although she was now the favorite of Agreda and the convent sisters, this was the age of the Inquisition. Mary de Agreda's Mother Superior insisted upon a rigorous ecclesiastical examination of her young novitiate. The Provincial of Burgos, Father Anthorn de Villacre, conducted the examination himself, and found that Sister Mary de Agreda had achieved a true sanctity usually reserved for saints.

During her trances, Sister Mary de Agreda began her mystical missionary journeys to America. She found herself preaching to large tribes of Indians in the deserts of another continent. She counseled them to travel to the village of Isleta in New Mexico. There they should ask for priests to come and further instruct them in the way of the one true faith. Sister Mary described America to Father Alonso Benvenides as a large island surrounded by the sea, rich in gold and precious stones. Still, she hardly knew what to make of its pagan indigenous people until an angel convinced her that they were humans with souls not unlike her own.

Sister Mary also saw into the future and watched as the Spanish priests attempted to convert these people. By simply raising her hand to God, she stopped arrows from hitting the missionaries. Her prayers softened the hearts of the pagans so that they more readily received Christ and the sacrament of baptism. When two priests were martyred in America, she marched in the procession carrying their bones to a chapel in a silver reliquary.

Sister Mary de Agreda's teleportations to the American Southwest continued regularly from 1620 to 1631, often three or four times a day, totalling about five hundred visits altogether. She claimed that during the visits she endured drastic changes in temperature and often saw the earth divided into night and day. Understandably, she was mentally and physically exhausted.

Satan continued to taunt her with persistent sexual temptations. In her dreams he presented her with diabolical images of her wickedness. During these times, God abandoned her and she descended into the realm of hell to wrestle with the devil. Each time she emerged victorious.

Even though she protested her unworthiness, the church saw her as holy and deserving of being named mother superior of her convent. At age twenty-five—so young that her appointment required papal dispensation—Mother Superior Mary de Agreda had to cope with the earthly functions of fund-raising for expanding the convent and feeding the poor, while continuing her missionary efforts on a higher level. Each time her administrative position came up for renewal, she begged for release from the earthly duties of being mother superior. This request was granted only once, from 1632 to 1635, when she served the convent simply as a nun. After that the church reassigned her to the burdensome office of mother superior, and she held the position until her death.

Mother Mary de Agreda constantly worried that her journeys were unreal and the work of the devil. She could never say for certain whether she made the journeys in spirit only, or whether she physically traveled to America. She seemed to believe that she made the trip in spirit with her guardian angel. To test herself, she decided to take rosaries to the Indians. Upon her return, she searched her cell but could not find the rosaries, and she concluded that she had physically gone to America. Later, priests would discover rosary beads among the tribes, which the Indians claimed were brought to them by the Blue Nun.

No indigenous people became more devoted to the Blue Nun than the Xumanos. Early Spanish padres applied the term *Xumanos*, or *Jumanos*, to the indigenous people who lived along the Rio Grande River in Texas, and who painted and tattooed their bodies, without regard for specific tribal designation.

Every summer for seven years, beginning around 1620, a delegation of Xumanos traveled to the Pueblo village of San Antonio de Isleta near

Albuquerque. They requested that priests come to their villages and baptize their new tribal members, just as the Blue Nun had urged them to do. The priests of Isleta, stunned at the sight of Native Americans reciting the catechism, asked how the Xumanos knew so much about the faith of the Roman Catholic Church, and the Xumanos proudly replied that the beautiful Lady in Blue had taught them. They were the first to make Mother Mary de Agreda's activities known to the Franciscan missionaries.

Intellectual Catholic missionaries found it hard to believe that a barely literate young girl could convey the complex dogma of the Roman Catholic faith to foreign heathens, even if she could visit them. Because of a shortage of priests on the New World Frontier and their disbelief in the stories of the Blue Nun, the padres of Isleta ignored the Xumanos' request for several years. Finally, in 1629, after Sister Mary's priests had failed to come and baptize them, several Xumanos revolted against those who believed the Blue Nun's teachings. During the insurrection she appeared before each rebel individually and begged him not to lose faith. No sooner had she ascended into the heavens than a scouting party returned with the news that the priests were on the way and would be there in only two days.

Sister Mary made a special return trip to help the Indians decorate wooden crosses with flowers so that they could present the priests with a proper Christian welcome. Fathers Juan de Salas and Alonso de Benavides were warmly greeted by a large procession of Xumanos carrying flower-bedecked crosses.

After their baptisms, the Xumanos accompanied the priests into other villages, where more tribes awaited the ambassadors of the Blue Nun. They all told the story of a visit by the beautiful Lady in Blue who carried a white cross. Not only were the priests surprised to discover that Indians knew so much about the Catholic faith, they were even more stunned to learn that a woman had arrived in the New World first.

Fathers Juan de Salas and Alonso de Benavides became so convinced that God had intervened for them through Sister Mary de Agreda that they took their stories back to Albuquerque, and then to Mexico City. While in Mexico City, Benavides asked the archbishop for permission to return to Spain to report on the activities of the Lady in Blue.

On August 1, 1650, Benavides described the series of events surrounding the Blue Nun to the commissary general of the Indies, Father Juan de Santander. Santander believed him and added a personal letter endorsing his observations. In his report to King Philip IV, Benavides subtly reminded the monarch that the mission fathers had discovered temporal as well as spiritual treasures in the New World. He hoped the lure of mineral wealth might induce the King to send more priests to New Spain.

Benavides described the amazing conversion of the Xumanos by the Lady in Blue, but did not name Sister Mary de Agreda because he didn't know her identity. Moreover, he had to be careful lest the Father General Fray Bernardo de Siena think him either mad or overzealous. He simply described her as a woman on whom God had bestowed the power of bilocation and the gift of speaking in tongues. During his audience with the father general, Benavides stammered while explaining the miracles that had been performed by a Spanish lady wrapped in a blue cloak on a Southwest desert thousands of miles away. Before Benavides could finish, Siena raised his hand and interrupted him:

> You need search no further. I can tell you who your Lady in Blue is. Several years ago it came to my attention that Sister Mary de Agreda had visions and revelations concerning the pagan tribes of New Mexico. [Arizona was then part of New Mexico.] What you tell me only confirms what I heard from Mother Superior Mary Agreda herself.

In 1630, Benavenides traveled to Sister Mary's convent and informed her that under the command of obedience to the church she was to reveal to him the details of her journeys to America. He tested her with questions about the landscape and people, which only someone who had been there could answer. Mother Superior Mary de Agreda humbly cooperated, replying with truthful, accurate answers. She told him of meeting with an Indian chief, blind in one eye and known to Benavides as Tuerto. On another occasion, with her own hands she had herded the Indians in an orderly manner into a small chapel and helped Father Cristobal Quiroz baptize them; when the Indians had looked back to see who was pushing them, they saw no one. She correctly described Friar Cristobal as having no gray hair and a ruddy complexion. She kept a diary of her visions and teleportations and showed Benavides the records of the times when the Arizona Indians had tried to strike her down with arrows.

Mother Superior Mary de Agreda was never certain how she came to be among the American Southwest peoples. She told Benavides that she had traveled on the wings of St. Michael and St. Francis and had been cared for by the ministrations of these guardian angels.

Benavides asked her why the Indians had the privilege of seeing her when the friars had not. Sister Mary replied that it must be that the Indians had the greater need.

Benavides attempted to investigate all the activities of Mother Superior Mary de Agreda, because he hoped that a revelation of her work might inspire the Spanish monarchy to provide more financial support to the Franciscan missions in the New World. Unfortunately, he never finished his research. Shortly after his first interview with Sister Mary de Agreda, the father general appointed him as a missionary to India. Benavides died while en route to his new post at Goa, India.

In a letter to the King Philip, Father Benavides described Mother Superior Mary Agreda:

> Mother Superior Maria de Jesus, abbess of the convent, is about twenty-nine years of age, handsome of face, very fair in color, with a light rosy tinge and large black eyes. Her habit and that of all the nuns in the convent is the same color as ours; that is, brown sackcloth, very coarse, worn next to the body. The nuns wear over the brown habit a white one with a scapular of the same material and the cord of St. Francis. They wear the rosary over the scapular; they have no shoes or sandals, other than boards tied to their feet. Their outdoor cloak is of blue cloth, coarse with a black veil.

Sister Mary was very tall for a woman of that time. When her bones were transferred to her final resting-place in 1909, she was described as having been about five feet, eight inches. Although she described herself as stout, she was light and quick and able to exert great strength in her performance of ordinary household tasks. Like most mystics, she seemed to suffer from a constant fever.

Sister Mary de Agreda wrote several books in addition to her diary. The most famous is her description of heaven in the *Mystical City of God*, which she insisted was based on descriptions that she received from the Virgin Mary. In fact, she wrote *The Mystical City of God* not once, but twice.

While Sister Mary's confessor, Father Francisco Andres de la Torre, was away, her childhood confessor took over de la Torre's duties. The old priest, Father Juan de Torrecilla, disapproved of nuns writing books. He ordered her to destroy her writings. Dutifully, she burned them. When de la Torre returned and discovered that *The Mystical City of God* had been destroyed, he became angry. He told Sister Mary that she had sinned by not consulting others, and that she must write the book all over again. (Talk about author-editor problems!) She did, but the task took her another ten years.

In 1627, Sister Mary de Agreda heard a voice order her to write the biography of the Virgin Mary. Despite the incident in which she had been told to destroy her diary and *The Mystical City of God*, she felt she had no choice but to acquiesce. This time she first received the blessing of Father de la Torre, who insisted that she obey the voice and write the biography.

When King Philip IV heard about *The Mystical City of God*, he requested a copy. Sister Mary demurred, but de la Torre supplied him with a copy. The king invited several prominent theologians to read it. They praised it so highly that the king insisted that she become his advisor in matters of the soul and state. For the next twenty-two years King Philip and Mother Mary de Agreda corresponded daily. The king wrote his questions on the left-hand side of the page and Mother Superior Mary Agreda replied on the right side.

When de la Torre became ill and died, Sister Mary's new father confessor learned of her writings, including the diary of her eleven-year missionary expeditions in America's Southwest. He ordered her to burn them all, and she once again obeyed without question. This father confessor died within three years. His replacement, Father Andres de Fuenmajor, attributed great significance to her writings and her work among the Indians. He renewed de la Torre's precept and ordered her to continue rewriting *The Mystical City of God* and her own autobiography.

During the last five years of her life, Sister Mary Agreda achieved the pinnacle of perfection in holiness and became renowned as one of the great mystics. On May 14, 1665, she collapsed while partaking communion. The sisters carried her to her cell, where she told them that her death was imminent. The public, having learned of her illness, poured out their grief before the convent in her final hours. Agreda's most revered cult image, Our Lady of Miracles, was brought to her bedside. It did Mary more harm than good: She violently protested that she was an unworthy creature.

On Thursday, May 21, her confessor, Father Andres de Fuenmajor, administered to Mary the Extreme Unction, which gave her a measure of peace. On May 24, Whitsunday—the traditional day of the descent of the Holy Ghost—the nuns and several priests chanted the Creed as her soul was borne away. Those in attendance of the Venerable Mary of Jesus de Agreda heard her declare, "Come Holy Ghost."

After her death, Sister Mary's book *The Mystical City of God* once again stirred civil and ecclesiastical controversy, particularly because in the book the mother of Jesus described the world as round, with poles at either end. This was heresy. The Spanish Inquisition examined the book for fourteen years and placed it on its forbidden book list for three months. The Grand Inquisitor ultimately agreed that the truth of Sister Mary's experiences might be questionable, but no blame could be placed on her intentions.

Spiritual fraud was a serious offense; another nun had been given two hundred lashes and life imprisonment for making false spiritual claims. The Inquisition doubted that Sister Mary, a simple country girl, could have produced a complicated work of theology. Nevertheless, the great universities of Spain hailed it as a brilliant work, while the French Sorbonne decried it as Scotist-Franciscan.

In 1694, more than sixty-four years after Sister Mary de Agreda's visitations to the American Southwest, Captain Juan Mateo Manje accompanied the great Jesuit missionary Father Eusebio Francisco Kino on an exploration of the Gila River in present-day Arizona. Kino and Manje, the first Europeans to visit the area, heard stories of the Blue Nun from the Yumas, the Cocomaricopas, and the Pimas, the last of whom lived at Casa Grande, not far from the present-day Arizona town of the same name.

The Pimas told Manje and Kino that the Blue Nun, wrapped in a cloud so bright it momentarily blinded them, had descended upon them from a great height, wearing a long brown robe covered by a blue mantle and a cloth or veil over her face. They related that their elders had pierced the Blue Nun with arrows and left her for dead twice. When they approached to examine her body, she levitated to the heavens, scolding them for not accepting the one true faith and scaring them into Christianity.

Evidently, Sister Mary was not entirely without a temper; the Pimas complained that she shouted and harangued them in a language they could not understand. Why God did not give her the ability to be understood to these Indians is a mystery. Perhaps in this instance Satan was able to confound her work.

In modern-day Mexico and the American Southwest, Hispanics and Native Americans often wrap their dead in a blue shroud in honor of Sister Mary Agreda. In Arizona her image has been seen in the gnarled roots of a mesquite tree, in the rust of leaking water pipes, and in many other unlikely places. From Madrid to Mexico to Arizona, she continues to visit the distressed, the sick, and the dying, performing miracles of healing and charity.

We will likely never know if the words and visits of the Blue Nun were real, but it doesn't really matter to those who believe. The Lady in Blue helps them through danger and illness, and bestows gifts from heaven, and that is more than enough.

chapter 14

The Miracle of the Roses

And there appeared a great wonder in heaven; a woman clothed with the sun, and the moon under her feet and upon her head a crown of twelve stars. . . . And she brought forth a man child who was to rule all nations.

—Revelation 12:1

Our Lady of Guadalupe joins La Llorona and the Blue Nun in the triumvirate of feminine souls who have had a profound spiritual influence on Arizona history. Like La Llorona, Our Lady of Guadalupe originated in Mexico, though she appears throughout Latin America and the American Southwest; like the Blue Nun, her image has appeared in the most unlikely of places—on rusty drainage pipes, in mesquite tree hollows, spray painted on cars and boarded-up windows.

In Arizona, New Mexico, Colorado, Texas, and Latin America, many Roman Catholic churches have been named in honor of Our Lady of Guadalupe. In 1750, Pope Benedict XIV granted Our Lady of Guadalupe her own feast day, December 12, on which her faithful devotees throughout

Arizona and the Southwest serenade her, visit her altars, and throw parties for girls named after her. In the 1920s, when the Yaqui Indians fled to Arizona from Sonora, Mexico, they called their new village Guadalupe; Our Lady of Guadalupe is their patron saint.

Believers in Our Lady are fiercely protective of her, as Maricopa County officials found when they sought to oust her from St. John Vianney, a poor Avondale church. Members of the church, under the leadership of Father Joe Coppora, Father John Herman, and the Salesian Sisters of St. John Bosco, cleaned up tons of trash from a vacant lot across from the church building. They took a place where people came to torch cars and do drugs and made it into a safe, clean park. Father Coppora wanted to move a storage center to the park for use as a youth center. County officials offered to help, with a few conditions. The church would have to add a separate handicapped exit and restroom, redo the wiring, provide architectural drawings, and get in line for a monumental number of government permits. The priests would also have to get rid of the Lady of Guadalupe—separation of church and state, don't you know? The last condition was too much. The church kept Our Lady of Guadalupe.

As described in the book of Revelation, Our Lady of Guadalupe wears a gold crown, and a blue robe sprinkled with stars. She stands on a crescent moon supported by a tiny angel. Her entire body is surrounded with a brilliant emanation. She is usually depicted as she is in Mexico City's Basilica: dark-skinned with tender, downcast eyes, her hands in an attitude of supplication.

The miracle of roses that brought this Madonna to remote desert regions occurred centuries ago. On August 13, 1521, after a long bloody battle, Hernán Cortés captured Mexico for the Spanish crown. Three years later, Franciscan priests arrived to convert the Aztecs for the cross. An Aztec man named *Quauhtlatoatzin* (he who speaks like an eagle), from the village of Cuaitlan, was among those who were converted. With the Christian name Juan Diego, he and his wife, Maria Lucia, were baptized in 1524.

Juan Diego was a poor Indian who did not belong to any of the Aztec castes, but he was not a slave, either. The fact that his Aztec name ended in *tzin* indicates that in earlier times he would have enjoyed a fair measure of prestige among his people. After the conquest, he farmed a small piece of land and made fiber mats to eke out a living. When Maria Lucia died in 1529, he moved in with his uncle, Juan Bernardino, to take care of the ailing old man.

Juan Diego was noted for his devotion and piety. Every weekend, in all kinds of weather, he walked barefoot to Mexico City to attend Mass and receive religious instruction. On cold mornings he wore a mantle known as a *tilma,* which he had woven from coarse maguey fibers. Only the wealthy could afford leather or fiber sandals and cotton clothing.

One early, cold December day in 1531, Juan Diego trudged through the snow on his way to Mexico City. At dawn he heard beautiful mellow voices singing in a strange language at the top of Tepeyacac Hill, which in ancient times was sacred to the Aztec goddess Tonantzin. Juan Diego asked himself, "How should I, a poor peasant, be so fortunate as to hear such beautiful music? Perhaps I have died and gone to heaven."

Juan Diego looked up the hill in the direction of the divine chant, and the music stopped. Suddenly there appeared before him a beautiful, olive-skinned Madonna surrounded in a ball of light as brilliant as the sun. Her garments sparkled with celestial grandeur. He marveled at her presence, but felt no fear, and fell to his knees in devotion.

She spoke to him in a soft gentle voice, using his native tongue of Nahuatl: "Blessed Juan Diego, most humble man of God, where are you going?"

Juan Diego replied, "Blessed Mother of God, I go to your temple to receive instruction in the ways of your son."

She replied, "You know well that I am the Holy Mary, Mother of the True God. Go before Bishop Juan de Zumarraga and ask him to build a temple on this spot so that I may give all my love, compassion, and protection to my flock. Here I will hear their cries for help and remedy their miseries and afflictions. Have no fear, for I am with you."

Juan Diego asked, "Who am I, a poor peasant, a nobody, that the bishop should heed my words?"

"God will be with you," she answered, and with those words she disappeared.

Juan Diego went to Mexico City and pleaded with Bishop Zumarraga's servants to announce him. Finally they went before the bishop and insisted that a crazy Indian wanted to see him. Should they send him away? The bishop thought for a few moments and advised his servants that he would see Juan Diego.

Bishop Juan de Zumarraga was born in the Basque country around 1468. He had entered the order at a tender age, and on December 6, 1528, the king ordered him to leave for New Spain without consecration. He became the first bishop and then the first archbishop of New Spain. Although he was paternalistic and authoritarian toward the Aztecs, he strenuously defended them against mistreatment by the Spaniards. His contemporaries roundly criticized him for his solicitude.

The bishop listened patiently to the Indian's incredible story and then said, "You will return at a later time, my son, and I will give thought to your wishes."

The next week, Juan Diego again climbed through the snow up Tepeyacac Hill on his way to Mexico City. Again he experienced the apparition of the Madonna. Trembling with fear because he had failed in his mission, he prostrated himself before her. "Most Holy Mother, the bishop listened benevolently, but it appeared he did not believe me. Holy Mother, I have failed. Please entrust your message to someone more worthy."

The Holy Mother did not scold him, but said in a gentle voice, "I have many messengers, but it is for you to ask the bishop to build a temple on this spot. You have been chosen to go before the bishop. You go in my name. Tell him the Mother of God sent you."

He replied, "Gladly and willingly I will comply with your mandate. I will do your wish and hope that he will hear and believe me."

Juan Diego set out to attend Mass and to be instructed in divine matters. After the service, he again presented himself at the gate of the bishop's palace. After a long wait the servants reluctantly allowed him to see the prelate. As he knelt at the bishop's feet, he again expressed the Holy Mother's directive.

After his precise description of the Lady, the bishop said, "Yours is a sincere devotion, but we must have a sign."

Juan Diego said, "My Lord, tell me only what sign you require and I will ask for it from Our Lady."

"The Lady will know what sign to give you." With those words the bishop dismissed Juan Diego but ordered several trusted members of his household to follow him. After Juan Diego crossed the bridge to Tepeyacac Hill, he disappeared from their view and they could not find him again.

They returned to the bishop and told him he had been deceived. They asked him not to believe what Juan Diego said. The bishop said nothing. Among themselves they plotted to beat the Aztec if he returned.

When Juan Diego again met the Lady, he told her the words of the bishop. She said, "Tomorrow I will give you a sign for the bishop. Return tomorrow at this time."

On the day when Juan Diego was to meet Our Lady, his uncle became very ill. Juan Diego summoned a doctor, who said it was too late. Better he should summon a priest to hear his uncle's final confession. The time with the doctor kept Juan Diego from his appointment with the Lady.

The next morning, Juan Diego rose early to summon a priest. As he approached Tepeyacac Hill, he worried that if he proceeded forward the Lady would detain him and it would be too late to call a priest. Suddenly she appeared in front of him. "Whither goest my son?"

Juan Diego dropped to his knees. "Blessed Mother, my uncle is near death and I hurry to get a priest so that his soul may enter heaven. I beg your forgiveness for the grief I have caused the most Blessed Virgin. After I have found a priest and brought him to my uncle, I shall deliver your message. I do not deceive you."

"Hear me, my son. Nothing shall frighten or grieve you. Do not fear for your uncle, who is under my protection. Let not your heart be disturbed. At this very moment he is cured."

When Juan Diego heard these words from the Blessed Mother, he was greatly relieved. "Thank you, Blessed Mother. Now I must hurry to the bishop with your message. Please give me the sign by which he shall believe me."

"Gather roses of Castile in your mantle and present them to the bishop. Show them to no one else. Tell him that they are a gift from the Lady of Guadalupe. There are many I could send, but you are my most worthy ambassador." With those words the Blessed Mother disappeared.

Juan Diego wondered where he would find roses on such a cold winter day. The mountain was over a mile high and had very little growth of any kind. Juan Diego looked up, and where the Holy Virgin had stood in the snow, there now bloomed a bush, full of beautiful red roses.

Confident of her care, Juan Diego gathered the roses in his mantle. He hurried to the city and went straight to the house of the bishop. When he insisted on seeing the prelate, the servants first pretended not to hear him. Then they said he was too early, or too late. They did not dare lay their hands on him, for they knew he was protected.

Finally Bishop Juan de Zumarraga's secretary told the priest, "That crazy Indian is here again to see you. Shall I have him arrested?"

The bishop thought for a moment and said, "Show him in. I will hear his petition."

Juan Diego entered the massive quarters and dropped to his knees before the bishop. "Father, the Blessed Mother has sent you a gift of roses from the mountain."

"My son, how can there be roses in the mountain snows at this time of the year?"

As Juan Diego dropped his cloak, the roses cascaded to the floor at the bishop's feet. Zumarraga's court gasped. They were even more amazed when they saw the image of the Holy Virgin imprinted on the cloth of Juan Diego's mantle. The bishop and his court dropped to their knees before Juan Diego. The bishop gently removed the mantle and begged Juan Diego's forgiveness for not believing him.

Juan Diego remained in the bishop's house for the night. The next morning he and the bishop set out for Tepeyacac Hill with a retinue of servants. After Juan Diego pointed out the site where the Holy Mother wished to have her temple built, he begged leave to go to his uncle, Juan Bernardino. The bishop refused to let him go alone and set out with him.

When they arrived, they found Juan Bernardino happy and healthy. He, too, was visited by the Holy Mother, and she healed him. Juan Bernardino testified that he learned through her that she had sent his nephew to Mexico City to see the bishop. Moreover, he said that she told him to "Call me and my image Santa Maria de Guadalupe." From that day forth the Holy Mother became known in Mexico as Our Lady of Guadalupe.

After the miracle of the roses, Juan Diego moved into a chapel room where he cared for the sacred image of Our Lady of Guadalupe until his death on May 30, 1548, at the age of seventy-four. The average life expectancy for men at the time was less than forty years.

⚜

Madonnas are generally named for the site where they appear, and so the name "Guadalupe" is controversial. Its origin is shrouded in mystery, though some believe it may be a translation of *Coatlaxoeuh,* which means "she who crushes the serpent" in the Aztec language of Nahuatl. The Aztec snake god had demanded human sacrifices, including those of babies and children, and some believe Our Lady of Guadalupe desired to crush this practice. Today she is called upon as a protectress of children.

Others believe the name came from Spain, which has its own Lady of Guadalupe, one among that nation's myriad of apparitions. Spain's Our Lady of Guadalupe began appearing in the Spanish province of Extremadura, home of the conquistadors Cortés, Alvarado, and Pizzaro. She appeared in Latin America even before 1531.

In 1533, Bishop Zumarraga celebrated Mass at the first Basilica of Our Lady of Guadalupe, where Juan Diego's mantle was given a place of honor during a religious procession. On the day of the dedication, an Indian was shot in the neck with an arrow and killed; when his body was placed before the image on Juan Diego's mantle, he was immediately restored to health. Thus the Lady began a long and impressive series of miracles, which continues to this day throughout Mexico and the Southwest.

In 1571, Admiral Doria carried a copy of Our Lady's image aboard his ship during the battle at Lepanto. He attributed his victory over the Ottoman Empire to the Virgin of Guadalupe. That same year the historian Juan de Tovar transcribed the story of Our Lady of Guadalupe from Zumarraga's writings in his *Primitive Relation.* On January 16, 1667, the archbishop of Mexico ordered that Juan Diego's mantle be enclosed in a glass case to prevent people from kissing it or pressing rosaries against it. By the mid-eighteenth century, all of New Spain, which included Arizona, accepted the patronage of Our Lady of Guadalupe.

In 1810, Our Lady of Guadalupe became a political symbol when Mexico fought for its independence from Spain. The revolution proclaimed life to the Dark Virgin and death to the Spaniards, and Our Lady's image appeared on the banners of Miguel Hidalgo and his troops. Naturally, when Mexico was victorious, the success was attributed to Our Lady of Guadalupe, although she must have endured relentless consternation during this revolution—the royalists claimed the support of the Virgin of Remedios, and from time to time the two armies shot each other's virgins.

In 1921, a bomb placed beneath an image of the Virgin exploded. Great damage was done to the Basilica, but no harm came to the image. Eight years later, the official photographer of the old Basilica of Guadalupe, Alfonso Marcue, discovered an apparent reflected image of a bearded man believed to be Juan Diego in the right eye of the Virgin. The church ordered him to keep quiet about his discovery, and he obeyed.

In more recent times, certified eye doctors discovered the appearance of human figures in the corneas of both of the Virgin's eyes. Dr. Rafael Torrija Lavoignet noted that her eyes looked strangely alive when he examined them.

In 1945, Pope Pius XII pronounced Our Lady of Guadalupe to be the Queen of Mexico and the Empress of the Americas. He said that she had been painted "by brushes that were not of this earth."

Today Our Lady of Guadalupe is a powerful religious symbol not only for Mexico; her miracles have spread all over the Western Hemisphere. She remains a symbol of hope for the poor and downtrodden.

References

ARTICLES

Brown, Carol Osman. "A Grand Old House," *Phoenix Magazine* (April 1977): 56–57.

Daniels, Steve. "Legend Still Reigns at Death Trap Mountain," *Los Angeles Times* (10 January 1985).

Eppinga, Jane. "Ethnic Diversity in Arizona's Early Mining Camps," *History of Mining in Arizona* 2 (1991): 49–73.

Hillerman, Tony. "Navajos Call Them Skinwalkers," *New Mexico Magazine* (July 1992): 66–67.

Leddy, Betty. "La Llorona in Southern Arizona," *Western Folklore* 2 (1948): 272–277.

McDonald, James F. "The Lost Dutchman," *Arizona Daily Star* (25 February–3 March 1912).

Morris, Robert L., Stuart B. Harary, Joseph Janis, John Hartwell, and W. G. Roll. "Studies of Communication During Out-of-Body Experiences," *The Journal of the American Society for Psychical Research* 73, no. 1 (1978): 79–94.

Neldon, Gail. "Weird Tales at Williams High School," *AFFword* vol. I, no. 1 (1968): 12–19.

Osis, Karlis and Erlendur Haraldsson. "Deathbed Observations by Physicians and Nurses: A Cross-Cultural Survey," *The Journal of the American Society for Psychical Research* 71, no. 3 (1977): 153–168.

Quinn, Ron. "Treasure Trails: the Apparition in Carmen," *Southern Arizona Trails* (May 1988): 22.

Roach, Joyce Gibson. "The Legends of El Tejano the Texan Who Never Was," *Western Folklore* 27, no. 1 (1968): 14–15.

Shaffer, Mark. "Defendant is Acquitted of Murder: Flagstaff Worker was Slain," *The Arizona Republic* (20 July 1988).

BOOKS

Agreda, Mary. *The Mystical City of God.* 4 vols. Translated by Fiscar Marison. Albuquerque: Corcoran Publishing Co., 1914.

Antti, Aarne and Stith Thomson. *Tale Types of the Folktale.* Bloomington: Indiana University Press, 1949.

Baker, Betty. *Great Ghost Stories of the Old West.* New York: Four Winds Press, 1968.

Blackman, W. Haden. *The Field Guide to North American Hauntings.* New York: Three Rivers Press, 1998.

Blue, Martha. *The Witch Purge of 1878: Oral and Documentary History in the Early Navajo Reservation Years.* Navajo Oral History Monograph Series No. 1. Tsaile: Navajo Community College Press, 1988.

Bolton, Herbert Eugene. *The Rim of Christendom.* New York: The MacMillan Company, 1936.

Brownell, Elizabeth R. *They Lived in Tubac.* Tucson: Westernlore Press, 1986.

Colahan, Clark A. *The Visions of Sor Maria de Agreda: Writing Knowledge and Power.* Tucson: University of Arizona Press, 1994.

Davis, E. Adams. *Of the Night Wind's Telling.* Norman: University of Oklahoma, 1946.

Dunning, Charles H. *Arizona's Golden Road.* Phoenix: Southwest Publishing Company, Inc., 1961.

Erdoes, Richard. *Legends and Tales of the American West.* New York: Pantheon Books, 1991.

Fuller, John G. *The Great Soul Trial.* Toronto: The MacMillan Company, 1969.

Garcez, Antonio E. *Adobe Angels: Arizona Ghost Stories.* Truth or Consequences: Red Rabbit Press, 1998.

Goff, John S. *Arizona Territorial Officials.* Vols. 1–7. Cave Creek: Black Mountain Press, 1975–1998.

Granger, Byrd H. *Arizona Place Names.* Tucson: University of Arizona Press, 1973.

Griffith, James S. *Southern Arizona Folk Arts.* Tucson: University of Arizona Press, 1988.

Haile, Berard. *Legend of the Ghostway Ritual in the Maile Branch of the Shootingway, Part 1. Suckingway: Its Legend and Practice, Part 2*. St. Michaels: St. Michael's Press, 1950.

Janvier, Thomas A. *Legends of the City of Mexico*. New York: Harper & Brothers, 1910.

Kendrick, T. S. *Mary of Agreda: The Life and Legend of a Spanish Nun*. London: Routledge & Kegan Paul, 1967.

Lockwood, Frank C. and Donald W. Page. *The Old Pueblo*. Phoenix: The Manufacturing Stationers, 1930.

Lovelace, Leland. *Lost Mines and Hidden Treasure*. New York: Ace Books, Inc., (n.d.).

Murray, Earl. *Ghosts of the Old West: Desert Spirits, Haunted Cabins, Lost Trails, and Other Strange Encounters*. Chicago: Contemporary Books, Inc., 1988.

Osis, Karlis and Erlendur Haraldsson. *At the Hour of Death*. New York: Avon, 1977.

Poole, Stafford, C. M. *Our Lady of Guadalupe: The Origins and Sources of a Mexican National Symbol, 1531–1797*. Tucson: University of Arizona Press, 1996.

Robson, Ellen and Diane Halicki. *Haunted Highway: The Spirits of Route 66*. Phoenix: Golden West Publishers, 1999.

Sacks, B. *Arizona's Angry Man: United States Marshal Milton B. Duffield*. Arizona Monographs. Tempe, Arizona: Arizona Historical Foundation, 1970.

Samaniego, Friar Joseph Ximenez, O. F. M. *Life of the Venerable Mary of Jesus of Agreda, Poor Clare Nun*. Translated by Rev. Ubaldus de Pandolf, O. F. M. Poor Clare Convent, Evansville, Indiana, 1910.

Schaafsma, Polly, ed. *Kachinas in the Pueblo World*. Albuquerque: University of New Mexico Press, 1994.

Seibold, Doris, ed. *Folk Tales from the Patagonia Area: Santa Cruz County, Arizona*. University of Arizona General Bulletin No. 13. Tucson: 1948.

Standard Dictionary of Folklore, Mythology, and Legends. Vol. 2. New York: Funk & Wagnalls, 1950.

Thompson, Stith. *Motif Index of Folk Literature*. Vols. 1–2. Bloomington: Indiana University Press, 1955.

Toor, Frances. *A Treasury of Mexican Folkways.* New York: Crown Publishers, 1947.

West, John O. *Mexican-American Folklore.* Part of the American Folklore Series. Little Rock: August House, 1988.

COLLECTIONS

Butler, K. L. The Little Beanshooter and the Padres: Witchcraft Accusations Against a Suckingway Practitioner and the Franciscan Friars of St. Michael's Mission to the Navajo. Unpublished Manuscript, Hayden Arizona Collection, Arizona State University, Tempe.

Castillo, José del. Folklore and Folkways. Collected as part of a WPA project during the Depression.

Charles Proctor Collection of Ghost Stories. Tubac Historical Society, Tubac, Arizona.

Garcia, Alex. Personal collection of ghost legends. Tucson, Arizona.

Haile, Father Berard. AZ 132; Box 18 typescript of the Suckingway. Special Collections, University of Arizona Library, Tucson.

Henning, Lloyd C. (1941) "Sheriff, Scholar and a Gentleman: Frank J. Wattron." Arizona Historical Society, Tucson, Arizona.

Material on Sister Mary de Agreda. Translations of Father Benavides Memorial of 1630 reporting on Sister Mary's visits to the Southwest are available from the Library of Congress, the New York Public Library, and the Academy of Franciscan History in Washington D.C.

Probate Case Number 58416 in the matter of James Kidd, Deceased.

Tenney, James Brand. (1929) History of Mining in Arizona. Unpublished Manuscript. Bureau of Mines, Tucson, Arizona.

The Wishing Shrine Ephemera File. Arizona Historical Society, Tucson, Arizona.

INTERVIEWS

Bleser, Nick. Interview by author. Tubac, Arizona, October 15, 1999.

Brown, Carol Osmond. Interview by author on the Frank Luke house. Tucson, Arizona, October 5, 1977.

Garcia, Alex. Interview by the author on La Llorona. Tucson, Arizona, November 13, 1999.

Davisson, Lori. Interview by the author on Apache Spirits. Tucson, Arizona, January 10, 2000.

Gaylord, George. Interview by the author on the Cochise Hotel. Tucson, Arizona, September 13, 1999.

Leavengood, Betty. Interview by the author on the descendants of the Aguirre family (who homesteaded the Buenos Aires Ranch) and the Kentucky Camp story. Tucson, Arizona, June 13, 1999.

NEWSPAPERS
James Kidd
   The Arizona Republic, April 7, 1964; June 9, September 14, October 3, 4, 1967; January 20, 1971.
   The Phoenix Gazette, April 16, 1964; February 3, July 14, 1967; October 19, 31, 1971.
Prescott Ghosts
   Prescott *Courier,* October 29, 1995
Brunckow Mine
   Tucson Citizen, June 5, 1874.
Chupacapras
   McNamee, Gregory and Luis Alberto Urrea, "Hellmonkeys from Beyond," *Tucson Weekly,* January 2, 1999.
Thunderbirds
   Tombstone Epitaph, April 26, 1890.